Illuminating Don Juan

Sacred Ceremonies with Carlos Castaneda's Teacher

Illuminating Don Juan

Sacred Ceremonies with Carlos Castaneda's Teacher

By Peter Marquis

Copyright © 2022 Peter Marquis

All rights reserved. No part of this book, in part or in whole, may be reproduced, transmitted, or utilized, in any form or by any means, electronic or mechanical, including photocopying, recording, or by any information storage and retrieval system, without permission in writing from the publisher, except for brief quotations in critical articles, books and reviews.

First Edition 2022, Pelorian Digital

Print: ISBN: 979-8-9868676-1-8

eBook: ISBN: 979-8-9868676-0-1

Cover and Interior Design by Richard Rasa

Dedication

I could never have written this book without help from many people.

Tata Kachora for choosing me to write about him.

Mario Medina for introducing me to Tata Kachora.

Gloria Munoz for being my goodwill ambassador with all shamans.

Richard Rasa for rescuing me as a writer and finishing the publishing.

Alfonso Lazcano (Poncho) for dedicated work.

Kim Larsen for her tremendous help.

Neal Alen for hard work and advice.

Also, my brother David and children Jamie and Michelle.

And thanks to the friends, including Steven, Kim, Tata Oso, Cecilia, Nico, and the many others who provided support, advice and research.

Contents

Preface XI
Prologue:
   The Story of the Earth, Grandfather Lizard, and Me 1
1. The Pilgrimage 5
2. Grandfather Lizard Is Going Solar! 25
3. The Enchanting Child 31
4. The Spring Dance 45
5. Spring Dance Ending 55
6. The Sun Shaman 63
7. The Interview 73
8. Don Fyo – Maya Shaman 87
9. Messengers 121
10. Sanctuaries 143
Epilogue: Still Beauty All Around 151
Afterword: Winter Solstice 153
Notes on mythology and the name Don Juan 157

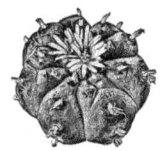

Preface

The purpose of this book is to take the mythical person known as "Don Juan" and show the world the real flesh and blood human. It is a brief look at his history, his ideas, and his humanity.

About fifty years ago, Carlos Castaneda delighted and captivated my generation with his novels about a sorcerer called Don Juan. Many of us believed Don Juan was a real person. I did. The first book is called: *The Teachings of Don Juan*. It is one of the most read books in the past fifty years. This book had a tremendous impact on my generation. The subject was even one of the favorite topics of debate during the early 1970s. Castaneda was doing research for a degree in Anthropology when he wrote the book. In it, he claims to have met Don Juan, a Yaqui Indian who was an expert on plants.

Don Juan was a Mexican *nahaul* or shaman. Castaneda's books were popular because they included his experiences with plants that have psychedelic effects, such as peyote. The books were released at the same time when many young people were beginning to experiment with psychedelic plant medicines.

The Don Juan character was fascinating as a person who

guided Castaneda through an apprenticeship that included psychedelic plants. He was old and wise and came from an exotic place that enchanted us.

This writer believes that a man called Tata Kachora is the person on whom Castaneda based the Don Juan character. Furthermore, he is alive and continues to behave the way he was described so long ago. Most people who do not read this book would never believe this story could be true.

Recently, I have had the chance to learn who I believe he really is. My goal is to share his message, as well as what I have learned about him. I hope I have gotten to the bottom of it. But while swimming at a lake bottom, a person only sees a little bit of something very big.

Tata Kachora has lived a very long life. He says he is 108 years old, yet he continues to travel to places as far away as Europe. No book, no matter how long, can capture all of the truth about the real Tata Kachora. Too much of his story is now shrouded in the misty past. However, he remains both larger than life and mysterious at the same time, and his message is one that comes directly from the Earth.

Prologue

The Story of the Earth, Grandfather Lizard, and Me

I was sitting at home temporarily trapped in 5 feet of snow, hoping it would melt before my second COVID shot in Yreka. I couldn't wait to head south to my sacred mountain in Mexico, called Pinacate. The COVID pandemic and the drought had kept me away for almost a whole year.

The phone rang, and it was Marco, my old assistant. After formalities, he tells me that he is a student of the greatest wizard of all time, and he never died. He asked me if I would like to meet him. The world knows him as a semi-fictional character called *Don Juan*.

Make no mistake: The real guy exists; it's just that his name is Grandfather Lizard in English. But in Spanish, his name is considered something of a title, and it is spoken as Tata Kachora. Now, everybody who knows him through literature or legend will immediately think that he can't be the one. Even if he wasn't a mythical character, he would be well over a hundred. But there is nothing impossible about this great wizard living to be over 107. In the books written by Carlos Castaneda, he told us that the last battle he had to wage was against old age. His father was a Yaqui Indian general, and he knew his birth date. He just had his birthday party with family and friends. It's an open secret.

But this is really a story of how we are trying to protect the Earth. The Earth just chose Grandfather and me to tell the story.

I am an old "head" from the 1960s who has evolved into an environmentalist. And he, the great *nagual* or wizard, has also evolved into an environmentalist. It's that simple. We are who we are. Take it on faith until the full picture becomes clear through my writing and pictures.

Note: Without pictures and eyewitnesses, people who don't know me well would think many of my stories are BS.

I don't need to put him through the same birth certificate scam as Obama because nobody fools me for long. He is the man! The irony is that the books from the past only hint at his greatness because Castaneda focused on psychotropic plants like peyote instead of the man and his actual teachings.

1

THE PILGRIMAGE

Many people dream of being a pilgrim. Some of us are lucky enough to go on a minor pilgrimage. I saw this as a gift equal to a Catholic being invited to meet the Pope. (Sorry, Francis! I do love you, but we are not from the same denomination.)

After getting the invitation from Marco, Gloria and I got ready. I brought some mushrooms since Marco had never tried them. I was curious about Marco's reaction to mushrooms, and how that might impact his impressions about the Castaneda books and the no longer mysterious Don Juan.

Gloria is my girlfriend and was born in Mexico. She is a beautiful woman who has lived in this magic town, Mt. Shasta, longer than me. Her hair is dark and wavy, and at first, her Native American features made me fail to realize that she is very light-complected. (When we travel in Mexico, people always ask her where she is from, and when she answers that she is from Jalisco, the standard response is something like, "Oh, that's where you get your light complexion from.")

She has a really sweet personality and is open-minded. I need her. She is able to translate Spanish that I can't quite understand. She also has a magnetic appeal to medicine men. I don't know that I would get past their front door without her.

Grandfather Lizard is an environmentalist! The other Grandfathers are environmentalists too. What did you expect? Of course, Grandfather Lizard has evolved in the last 50 years (which is how long it's been since "Pinche Carlitos"– Kachora's impolite nickname for Castaneda – was his black sheep student).

I had been feeling guilty for not accomplishing much lately. I'm basically a lazy ass who was spending too much time working on growing good bud. My only excuse was that I was old enough to be retired and was waiting for something important to do – a job worthy of my time, a sign from the Earth.

Gloria and I were already vaccinated, so we left the COVID epidemic behind. We headed to the border, excited to meet the great wizard. Marco was ready to go. I stupidly thought, "He is so old; what if COVID kills him before I can meet him?" So we hauled our asses and were at his house two days later.

We wound our way up to his wizard-looking house on top of the turquoise volcano. When I saw the shining house with its witch's hat turret, I started getting nervous. I had made a gamble. I had smoked on the way from the hotel. I needed my weed, but I figured he would not like it. Would it all be too much? Parking in the dirt lot, we got out and were quickly investigated by the dogs. We love dogs, and they sense we are ok.

There were beautiful people protecting Grandfather

Lizard. There was even a layer of beautiful dogs. The dogs are sweet and have magic markings like the pit bull with the pirate's patch or the little mutt with an arrowhead between her ears.

The grounds were lovely. There were organ pipes, senita or "old man" cacti, and the psychedelic San Pedro cacti. We wandered around, feeling more and more comfortable. A young woman (possibly in her twenties, with lovely black hair looking like many other young women here) appeared in between a large house and a low-slung building. She said her father would be ready in a few minutes, and we could continue waiting in the gardens.

The whole area is tranquil and serene. His little ranch reminds me of my own. It's in the mountains, and the neighbors are far enough to provide privacy. It is roughly 900 miles south of my place in Mexico. We both chose our locations carefully. Both are places of natural beauty. We both made the perfect choices. We will die in our beloved communities someday.

I had honed my taste while serving as a board member for my town's respected environmental center. I'll interject here with a memory of listening to the other board members stumble on a question like, which is worse – global warming or chemtrails? Ok, here is the answer: Jet exhaust, or what they call "chemtrails," is a contributing factor, but it is not very different from car exhaust. It all contributes to global warming. So unless they are cloud seeding, it is just jet fuel exhaust. Why would they want to kill all of us slaves? They don't put shit in the fuel to poison us with chemtrails. If you want to see someone who is poisoning us, go look in the mirror. I did, and that's when I went big on solar!

Here's where my ego wants to go self-righteous and

say, "You assholes fucked up my Earth." But I am still one of you! Driving all over the place, heating my house with diesel fuel. I am a fool too! But Grandfather Lizard is not as foolish as we are. The moment that I have, somehow, waited for all my life has arrived. The young woman comes out of the big house surrounded by precious little dogs. She bids us come and enter the small building, which is actually Grandfather Lizard's separate little house. The dogs trot over to the house. They are so polite that they scatter out of the way when we enter through the door. This door had been open the whole time, and we knew he could watch us from the dark space inside if he felt like it.

We leave the sparkling sunlight and walk through that door into his world. The room is his office filled with a hundred years old relics and photos - a real magical 107-year-old wizard's house! My Native American grandson loves my "magic house" and feels lucky when I let him play with my dolls. Now I am in my grandson's shoes! The room is full of magical stuff. He even has a picture of his dad, a general in Pancho Villa's Army. There is an opening into a darker room next to a small wood stove.

He appears in space! No cane, standing straight, with long white hair tied back. He is beautiful to my eyes. He appears to be over a hundred years old. Interestingly, he is dressed in a red shirt that says, "Free Leonard Peltier." (Peltier is the Sioux Indian who was imprisoned because of his alleged role in killing an FBI agent during the 1970s – A Wounded Knee Rebellion)

Grandfather invites us to sit in the three plastic lawn chairs in the middle of the room. I end up directly in front of him. My hair is long, like his. I am wearing a Zapatista shirt. We match in some way! Our shirts speak volumes if you have read the books behind them. Beautiful synchronicity!

Tata Kachora, Gloria and me

He is polite, but at first, he appears a little uneasy with my presence and doesn't understand my Spanish. He waves me away.

I'm not too surprised or disappointed, so I decide, "That's fine. What a better place can there be to just sit and observe." No longer nervous; I am just enthralled. He places his attention on my charming companions. Gloria is so beautiful that she quickly charms him, and vice versa. Marco reminds him that he is one of his students but has been studying from a different teacher for the past few years. The grandfather appears to remember him. He asks Marco about his progress, then invites him to the Spring Dance. Of course, Marco accepts. He is not a man with much dementia.

This book is my story. Please don't come up to me someday and ask the 50-year-old question, "Is he real?" Scholars have been debating this topic for 50 years. This is 2021, and last time I checked, he was real.

Ram Das said, "Be here now." The teachers are here. Listen to the Dalai Lama, Pope Francis, and Grandfather. They are all real!

Tata Kachora then introduces us to his dogs, pointing out the black eye patch on his friendly little pit bull called Pirate. I point out an arrow marking on the little mutt licking me. This dog is called Arrow. He nods in approval. This is the first time my direct communication has been successful. By now, I feel as if I am on peyote, mushrooms, or something. This man's energy is incredibly uplifting to me. As he once explained to a former student, "I don't have to take much anymore. I'm already there." So am I!

As he turns his curiosity to me, something is changing.

"Are you married?"

I answer in Spanish, "*Somos novios.*" (We are boyfriend and girlfriend.)

He understood me again. He asks if we have kids.

Gloria says, "I have two from my former marriage."

I encourage her to tell him that her daughter is an astrophysicist. When she tells him, he says, "fucking cool!" with a thumbs up. He would like to meet her. There aren't too many Latina astrophysicists.

He turns towards me and asks, "How many kids do you have?"

I tell him, "I have two children with different mothers." Then he looks wistfully into space and tells us that he has fathered 45 children and has been widowed four times. He is looking for wife number five.

He misses all of them, pointing out pictures on the wall. They were beautiful women from a world I will never understand. That world is all gone now." A deep sadness hangs over the room for a few moments. This is a common theme for him.

He looks straight into my eyes, "Why have you come here?"

"I am here to meet you because I know who you are, and it is a great honor."

"Thank you."

He stares at me, waiting, "But is there something else?"

My moment has arrived. I step up to him and explain that I heard him teaching other people about stopping polluting Mother Earth. He nods. I tell him that I have installed solar on my ranch, and I want to do the same for him to complete the circle.

"Solar power for the Grandfather! That is dope!"

He gives me a thumbs up and says, "*Chingon!*" "Fuck yeah!"

I sit back down. Wow, I think we are going to put solar on his house. I am poor, but it's not about the money. I will be paid back on some level. I never got paid for trying to save the Earth anyway. Real environmentalists don't get paid, well, unless they can write like Ed Abbey, you know. This is because we are threatening the big money interests.

For me, meeting Grandfather Lizard was meeting the single person on this whole planet whom I would want to meet the most. But I didn't know he was alive! His grace, dignity, and wisdom were there.

He looked at me then and asked if I do cocaine.

"No."

"Do you use heroin?"

"No."

"Do you smoke weed?"

I froze hesitantly, then said, "Yes." Between the weed, his tea, and his presence, I was very high.

"Oh, that isn't too bad. I don't mind it."

Although I didn't realize it, I was being interviewed! I was passing his tests. But where was this all going? Was Grandfather still so wise that he had a plan? After all, the Toltec Grandfathers still consider him to be the greatest! 107!

He offers us some tea brewed from a powerful medley of life-enhancing plants that he had gathered. He attributes his longevity to this tea. He sells this tea for $200 US dollars a kilo! I realized this was a way to honor him, as well as increase my own health, so I purchased a kilo from him. It tastes very pleasant, and drinking it does give me a sense of well-being.

He is reminiscing about his past and tells us that no one ever penned down his life story. "Pinche Carlos" didn't. He tells us that some people who interviewed him about plants didn't even go to see the plants. Apparently, they just filmed him talking. He looked at me and asked if I could do it. It was surreal, yet real. I was now agreeing to work with him and to do it his way. A big part of me didn't believe what had happened. Later in the car, I asked Gloria if he had really asked me to do all that. Yes, he had. My companions both agreed.

I'm now at home documenting what I have learned, getting ready to go put solar on Grandfather Lizard's house. Marco already knows the best solar engineer in northwestern Mexico. We will work on that first. But this has already turned into something much bigger.

I had already agreed to lead a pilgrimage to my sacred mountain. Some of Grandfather Lizard's students have heard of the mountain, and they asked me to take them. Grandfather Lizard talked about the Pinacate volcano in a book fifty years ago. It's another open secret, Pinacate, the great mystical volcano. I have been exploring the place since our aforementioned "bad student" wrote about it 50 years ago. I always sleep well in the beautiful arms of my sacred volcano.

Los Vidrios used to be a restaurant and motel. Built, I suspect, to house our astronauts in training for the moon landing. I am not kidding. The astronauts rode the world's first quad here, the lunar lander. Pinacate Volcano has a surface like a moon. But now, at Los Vidrios, only the ruins of the buildings remain!

This mountain is my sacred home.

The Native American population has been gone for 150 years, but they are returning. In a sense, the Desert People have already re-discovered their ancestral home. A leading shaman of the Tohono, O'odham, learned of Pinacate and is now holding ceremonies there. His people believe they were created by I'itoi, the fire god.

Gloria and I met the shaman named Kevin De La Cruz in a mystical way there last year. That meeting gave me final confirmation that I had "Medicine."

I'itoi must have arranged our meeting because it was truly magical. Now was my chance to pass the torch to the people who had been gone so long. The Tohono O'odham people who lived on the volcano had been hunted down, killed, and the survivors had run away to settlements in other areas. But now, they are rediscovering their roots. With the help of their own great shaman, they are learning the old ways and reclaiming their identity. They are holding ceremonies again.

When I am in Pinacate, I have decided to accept the premise that I'itoi is God. Like the goddess Pele is to the Indigenous Hawaiians, I'itoi is the volcano god, and he created the people. My personal relationship with I'itoi has led me to believe that "he" is somewhat of a trickster, kind of like a coyote. Many times I have been miles away from civilization, out in the wild, and things would go wrong. Fear sets in!

"Oh no. Can I make it back to the truck?"

"Oh shit! The old truck is broken. Can I make it back to

civilization?" Then suddenly, the clouds part, everything is now okay and resolved. It's beautiful and perfect again. I'itoi was only messing with me. Reminding me of the many blessings he bestows upon me. A bit of a trickster is the spirit of this mountain.

Gloria and I arrived on a windy day, so we drove past Pinacate and spent the night in the town of Puerto Peñasco. The town is a resort on the Sea of Cortez. The famous gangster, Al Capone, founded the town so he could smuggle liquor to Phoenix and Tucson during Prohibition. The first time I went to Puerto Peñasco was in the mid-1970s. It was a sleepy, little shrimp fishing village. We camped on the beach. Now, that beach is lined with luxury hotels.

I first met my friend Jesus there about ten years ago. He was standing in front of a store, inviting tourists to shop inside.

"Hey, buddy! We got everything you need: leather coats, clothes, carvings . . . do you need any weed?" I laughed and told him that my weed is ten times better than his.

"Oh shit. You got the kind?"

"Yeah, I got a little extra because I am crossing the border and need to get rid of it," I say. "I grew it on my ranch in the mountains of California." He had the kind of medicine I wanted, so we traded. We are friends now. Back then, his dream was to get his own store. Now he has his own drugstore. His wife and kids have moved down from Phoenix, and he is happy. He has to pay the mafia a thousand a month in protection money, but this is how things operate in Puerto Peñasco.

Gloria and I arrived in the late afternoon and rented a room in my favorite motel. It's in a part of town that has gradually filled with restaurants, hotels, and bars. It has grown seedy over the years. Prostitutes often stand on the corners. But people don't rob tourists. Without us, the town turns into a place of beggars with scarecrow faces.

Just before sunset, my enemy, the wind, disappears. Jesus walks over to our room from his nearby house. Following our normal routine, we rolled a couple of joints and walked over to the beach. The wind is gone, the beach is nearly deserted, and the sunset over Baja is spectacular. We have been driving for hours, and it feels great to walk on the beach. Gloria selects seashells. Somehow she always finds the most beautiful one. The tide is coming in, and we almost get trapped between the waves and the cement wall of Plaza de Las Glorias. I love Puerto Peñasco.

In the morning, we stop by the Tohono O'odham store. The owner is outside painting the front. His ponytail is even longer than the last time we met. We chat, and I tell him that we met the shaman he had been telling us about. He had shown us a picture of Kevin, the shaman, who was tall, handsome, and also had a long ponytail on his back.

This happened a year ago. We were on the way home, and we were driving by the volcano. We spontaneously decided to stop at the ranger station, as I hadn't eaten yet and wanted to fix a bowl of cereal. We also wanted the rangers to know that we had left the park, so we pulled off the highway and into the station parking lot. There were two interesting-looking men outside, next to a new Chevy truck. Curious, I addressed them in Spanish and asked if they were Indigenous.

"Si." A light starts to go on in my head!

"Do you speak in English?"

"Yes."

"Oh my god! Are you . . . ?" I searched for his name

when Gloria appeared and finished my question.

"Kevin?" They both nod yes. I'm stunned because we had just decided to visit the Tohono O'odham Reservation and drive to Sells, Arizona, to look for him. I wanted to meet him.

He, however, was here at the park headquarters. Of course! We should meet at the sacred mountain. My mind is racing. Would he understand?

"I know who you are. We are supposed to meet here," I gush. He nods skeptically, thinking: Who is this white guy confronting me? I kept talking, explaining that the guy at the store had shown us his picture, that I was the last old-timer left who knew many secrets of the volcano, that I was at his service. He just nods stoically, slowly grasping what I am telling him. He is wearing a white, long sleeve shirt and a white shell choker to contrast his black leather vest. His dark, piercing eyes are serious.

It turns out that the two are there for a ceremony. Later, they have a meeting with the Governor of Sonora to discuss illegal salt mining in the park. Kevin is an environmentalist. All shamans I know are environmentalists. We are connected to Mother Earth, so trying to preserve her comes naturally.

We are leading a spiritual revolution. People realize that our voices are speaking for the earth. We are voices from the past, the present, and the future. Grandfather is the best example of this.

Kevin and I stand there talking about the mountain. As I tell him about sacred places and artifacts, Gloria shows him pictures of some of them on her tablet. At one point, Kevin smiles at her and says she reminds him of his wife. High praise!

While we are talking, a red tail hawk flies past. The old Huichol worker named Jesus and his hawk has been silently watching the meeting. He seems to sense there is a passing of the torch, the importance of the moment. He operates heavy equipment and has worked in Pinacate for 25 years. He has been around shamans all his life. His people are known for their peyote pilgrimages. There is Medicine in the air.

Before we leave, Kevin's apprentice rolls a cigarette, and we hold a brief Tobacco Ceremony, passing the cigarette after blowing smoke ourselves. This is the way it is done.

Gloria and I left the meeting feeling elated. We had found Kevin! And he was just where he needed to be for a proper meeting. They are always there when we look for them, the shamans. We don't try to explain it anymore.

When we returned to the US on that day, it was because US customs had announced they were about to close the border. The COVID pandemic was getting bad. We had only gotten to camp one night. This time, we were fully vaccinated, and the border was open.

The park has been officially closed for years due to local politics. A skeleton crew remains at the ranger station, but the road has been blocked further on. We stopped to check in anyway. The closure does not affect us. We know about the road by the water tower that we can use to enter the park.

Before leaving the cell phone range, we check to see if there are any messages from Marco and the others. Still nothing. Where are those guys?

The next day we hike to the top of Red Cone, a beautiful little volcano where we have some cell phone reception. There is a cryptic message from Marco. He says there is criminal activity in the area. They are afraid to come. This is the first time in all these years that criminals have directly affected a Pinacate trip. We are safely nestled in the arms of Pinacate at Red Cone. My camp is secure. It is like my living room. No one goes to Red Cone anymore. It is the most beautiful part of the most beautiful place in the world, yet we are here alone.

The rains came late this winter, in mid-January. Nature doesn't care, and flowers have sprouted everywhere. The lavender and yellow flowers are already coloring the washes.

Little lupine sprouts abound on the slopes of black cinders. This year the sprouts will never grow as tall as the dead stalks they aim to replace. I scrape away the cinders with my boot, and they are wet about 2 inches down. If it doesn't rain again, at least the plants have enough moisture to grow for a few more weeks.

Yet on this trip, it is the animals who are back and putting on a show. My raven friends had seen my truck on the way in. They were probably watching our slow progress on the ancient, washed-out road, so they were at Red Cone watching us set up camp, waiting to be fed. I feel them, so I quickly prepare a meal for them, corn chips and nuts. They love me, and I love them. After they finish eating, they stand like black sentinels on the dark lavas above camp. They chortle contentedly like cats purring. This is my favorite sound in the world. Everything is perfect.

Sometimes when things are quiet, and the ravens are nearby watching us, I like to tease them. I say "boo" loudly, and it makes them flutter and jump for a second. I always laugh when they know they've been tricked. These birds are so smart that they actually have a sense of humor, and so they don't mind.

Red Cone (Pinacate) landscape

At some point, a red tail hawk began soaring between us and the red face of the rock. The ravens fly over and begin an aerial attack on the poor hawk. They dive-bomb her mercilessly. It's the only show in town! Then Gloria says, "Look, an eagle!" And sure enough, a golden eagle is high above watching the action. Eagles don't miss much. The scene is spectacular: black on red, as they fight in front of Red Cone. But it doesn't last long, and the eagle glides behind the volcano. The ravens tire of the attack, and everything is quiet again. It is always perfect when we visit Pinacate. I'itoi is good! The Earth is good! And even the weather report is good!

I never come in here if it is windy. One only has to check the forecast for Puerto Peñasco. In the old days, we used to come down without the weather forecast. Sometimes the wind would blow for four days. All you could do was hide from it. I hate wind more than anything. It will probably be windy on the day I die!

The wind is due to return tomorrow. The plan is to head back to the States and then drive to Tecate. Grandfather Lizard is waiting. We aren't too worried about whatever has happened on the highways because we can return to the US at the Sonoita Point of Entry. Outlaws would not dare to stop people on the road from Peñasco to Sonoita. It is the Golden Highway that brings the money to Puerto Peñasco. You don't allow anybody to rob the goose that lays golden eggs. We Gringos are this goose. No worries.

Before leaving Red Cone, I need to hold a ceremony. Years ago, I found a sacred rock and took it home. It is a shaman rock. Crystal clear, not quartz, about a pound. Earlier, I found a coin made from the same rock. It must have been very valuable to the Indians. I had planned to hold the ceremony with the shamans, but Marco and the others didn't show up. The idea was to return the rock and say a prayer for the Ancestors. So now I was to have the ceremony alone. Gloria was grouchy. Or maybe it was me.

I carried the rock using ancient trails through the lavas. Just before the sacred water holes or tinajas, I found an old trail. It was approaching the old village site from the east. The rock is there now! It may rest for another 200 years before another human touches it, surrounded by the barrel cacti, giant saguaros, creosote, and brittlebush, in the midst of all that beauty. Then I walked over to the old village site down to the pools of water, saying a prayer to the Earth, to I'itoi, I feel it!

I will soon be dust in the wind.

2

Grandfather Lizard Is Going Solar!

Marco told us that the outlaws had stopped every car on Highway 2 between four and six in the morning. They had stolen cars and robbed everyone. The one soldier who resisted was severely beaten. Marco and the others had also planned to use that highway. Sadly, Mexico was on the verge of becoming a failed state!

The wind had little impact on a heavily laden truck, and the glass provided protection. Perhaps, it's just the sailors who liked the wind.

The border crossing was uneventful. The border guard sensed that we were "normal tourists" and told us to pass after inspecting our passports. My tiny one-inch bottle of medicine was buried deep in the camping equipment. I had left the rest of my weed with Jesus and had no dog this time. Thank God! *Thank I'itoi! Thank Pacha Mama!* I knew they were all one and the same. They kept me safe.

Morning found us back in Yuma. An old friend, Frank, had just bought a home in one of those snowbird, double-wide, modular home parks. It was perfect for us. We blended in right away.

This time Marco showed up with his big Ford truck. We loaded up and headed for Baja and the home of Tata Kachora. The name Tata was a title bestowed upon a *nagual*, or shaman, when he had earned the full rank of Grandfather. Tata Kachora was the oldest and most respected of all the *naguals*. A Kachora, or lizard, is the keeper of the underworld. I hope the reader will understand that the past is irrelevant to Mexicans. Forget all the books written about Tata Kachora. He was our great shaman! The people came to him for healing. The whole concept of a medicine man never died in Mexico. They were often called *curanderos* or healers.

Gloria and I had visited her family in Mexico. Petra, her mother, was a *curandera*, and she lived with her ancient husband on the ranch where she was born. Locals often came to her for healing. People liked her because she could teach so much. Ironically, Petra and Tata Kachora had never heard of each other.

I had a friend whom I will discuss later. He was the powerful Maya shaman called Don Fyo.

He predicted what could happen to my family last year. I curse 2020 to hell with COVID, Trump, and death! I lost a stepson, a brother-in-law, an aunt, and others.

It was time to continue working on my dream of completing the circle and putting solar on Grandfather Lizard's house. The Earth had the plan, not me. I must remember this.

We entered Mexicali on a beautiful day. The wind was gone. Mexicali appeared to consist of piles of rubble and trash with houses interspersed. It was huge and filthy. One could easily understand how Tata Kachora evolved into an environmentalist. He saw the garbage everywhere and talked about it all the time.

After the checkpoint, Marco and I smoked a joint. We soon begin winding our way up into the high country of Baja.

The Mexican side of Baja was higher and more beautiful. A lot of it looked just like Joshua Tree National Park. You could buy land and live there. This was an option for me, as my cousin was buying my ranch. I had to leave it in 2 years.

We stopped in La Rumorosa to check out Marco's land. He was paying for a 4-acre plot. It was pretty, with giant granite boulders on top of hills. Pinyon pines, junipers, and wildflowers embroidered the landscape. I could live in Baja with fewer snowfalls in the mountains of Mexico.

Soon Marco maneuvered through the labyrinth that Tecate had become. We were almost there. Grandfather's son knew we were coming. However, it was afternoon and too late to visit. So tomorrow would be the day when we would see Tata Kachora.

Ensenada was only an hour and a half away. The highway winds through beautiful mountains, newly green from the rains. Giant trucks, belching diesel smoke, plied the highway. The highway became the Guadalupe Valley Wine Route. This region was Baja's version of Napa Valley, producing great wines and many millionaires.

Ensenada, it had been 25 years! Holy shit, it had turned into a big city! It shone in stark contrast to the slums of Mexicali. The downtown tourist area was fancy and upscale, resembling a Southern California city. It was safe and good for tourists. The 20-foot wide sidewalks were made of red tiles. There were hotels and motels everywhere. The dozens of cheaper ones all appeared to have red and green flashing neon signs that said, "Rooms for 280." That's about 14 US dollars. After inquiring, we learned that the 280 peso price only rents a room for about 8 hours, which was good enough for prostitutes and their clients. To rent a room until noon the next day was more like 22 US dollars. We rented rooms in the El Rancho Motel. It had one of those flashing neon signs but was attractive, and the rooms were clean.

While the maid was showing us the room, I settled into a chair with an odd shape. It was comfortable but had a strange narrow shape. It was all one piece and covered in vinyl. I commented that the chair was really comfortable to no one in particular. But the maid chuckled and told us that the chair was for trying new sexual positions. I jumped up and said, *"Bueno,"* which translates into "Well, okay then." Everybody shared a laugh over my innocence!

Next, we met at a restaurant with Poncho, a solar engineer. We immediately sensed our mutual connection, particularly over an interest in Fritjof Capra, whom we both admire and has strongly influenced us. Poncho soon became a good and respected friend. Arrangements were made for Poncho and me to bring solar power to Grandfather Lizard.

3

THE ENCHANTING CHILD

In the morning, we drove back to Tata Kachora's house and stopped for breakfast at a small restaurant nearby. We then wound our way up the hill to his family complex and parked across from his little house in the dirt lot. We slowly walked towards the steps leading to the family complex.

As I arrived at the bottom of the stairs, a woman, supposedly his daughter, and a small child, who I suspected was the grandson of Tata Kachora, appeared on the porch.

The child was beautiful, with big almond eyes, a ponytail, and a pendant necklace. The woman said, "This is my son."

So the big old Gringo said, "I understand. You're a boy like me, with a ponytail like mine." He continued to stare.

Gloria was next to me at the bottom of the stairs. While trying to understand the conversation between Gloria and the woman, my awareness returned to its place of origin, my body, and I noticed my space being invaded. The little boy was standing so close to my right side that he touched me. I looked down, and those big brown eyes were staring directly into mine with what could only be curiosity mixed with a desire to interact. To me, children were innocent and easy to understand. I had spent my entire adult life raising, teaching, and interacting with children. This one next to me was special. I had my eyes on him.

One by one, we wandered between the two houses and over to the "Waiting Wall." The sun had already warmed the temperature into the upper '50s. With no breeze, it felt so warm that there wasn't a need for a coat. March 1, 2021, was a gorgeous day, but my weather app predicted rain was coming.

After admiring Tata Kachora's cactus garden, I sat on the wall. Gloria and the boy came over and joined me. The wall was about 2 feet high, topped with wide gray bricks, and two-inch round steel poles stuck out every ten feet.

An old cellphone in the grandson's hand was his favorite toy. It still took pictures. He heard me mention that I had bought Marco a new phone. Those big, wistful brown eyes became melancholy as he said, "Nobody ever gave me a new phone." I had to give him the tired old explanation. He was too young, and they were expensive.

Gloria said, "This little girl is so cute, but she won't talk to me."

"That's because he is a boy, and you're calling him a girl."

"Really?" He was twirling around one of the metal poles, watching.

"Yes, he is a boy. You can tell."

She says in Spanish, "Oh, you are a boy?" He stared with those incredible eyes.

I got up and started speaking English to Gloria. The boy said, "I took your spot." Sure enough, he was in the spot

I had just vacated, looking gleeful. I immediately grasped what this game was about.

"Yes, you took my spot. Where is your spot?" He hopped up and went back to the pole, spinning around and pointing to his cellphone on top.

"Oh, ok."

The little dog named Arrow (remember her, the Arrow between her ears?) came up to me, and I started petting her. This distracted the kid, and he moved away from his spot. *It worked; the kid moved!*

I sat on his spot and said, "Look, I took your spot."

He smiled delightedly and sat where Gloria had just been.

"Look, I took her spot."

By now, my mind was blown because this game was straight out of his grandfather's first lesson. It had been in print for all to read for over 50 years. Tata Kachora's first lesson involved the student having to find their spot. All these years after the lesson took place, I was in front of his house with his grandson, and the child had turned it into a fun game. Was this DNA, or had Tata Kachora been teaching the same lesson for over 60 years? These people were legends. How lucky I was to be there.

Now that Gloria knew that he was a boy, he allowed her to interact with him. She asked his name. He stood there, touching her leg.

"Can I give you a hug?" she asked. He nodded yes. So she gave him a long hug and asked how old he was.

"*Cinco.*"

At 5, he was a year older than Gloria's grandson, Leo. Both boys were very cute. Leo called me Grandpa and didn't ask why I was white. The kids didn't notice color until an adult said something. The boy was interested in Leo and looked at pictures of him, saying, "I am a year older." Gloria was in love with the boy and couldn't help missing Leo. Back home, she usually had him on weekends, but not on this one.

Eventually, Tata Kachora's daughter signaled that he was ready to receive visitors. Gloria was still with Ian, so I wandered over to the door and peered into a room. He was standing in his spot at the end of the relic-covered table next to his chair by the bedroom. This was definitely his spot. He had bid me enter. My hair was in a bun this time; I didn't even know if he would remember me at 107.

There was a large peyote button in a pot on the table next to me. Even the peyote was still with him. It was all there. The spot and the peyote were from the first two lessons. (Every day, he still felt the pain of having somebody else making millions off of him and "not give me a penny!") He mentioned it every time he reminisced. So I took my chair in "my spot" next to the table. We were alone for the first time and waited, not knowing how to bridge the gap. I could feel him, feeling me, and vice versa.

It reminded me of the time I was in China in 1989. We had taken a boat up the Yangtze River to a remote Buddhist monastery that could only be reached by water. I got separated from my party and wandered around the monastery. I took pictures of a huge Buddha statue (the type where Buddha is sitting with his legs crossed, fat, and smiling benignly.)

As I got finished with the photos, a door behind the statue had opened, and from a dim light within, the silhouette of an old man appeared. He slowly entered the open stall with the statue and smiled at me. This man was the most ancient human I had ever seen. He was obviously the patriarch. So he motioned me to sit with him on some chairs next to the Buddha. I remembered his wise, ancient face. He had survived many wars and revolutions. In the 1970s, radical young people had come here to destroy traditions and "cleanse China." They had blown the corner off the Taoist monastery that I had hiked past upriver. You could still see the destroyed section, left to remind all those who saw it, screaming, "There was a war of culture here!" In the name of Mao's "Cultural Revolution," those hideous confused children had murdered wise old men.

The old man and I sat in silence for a few minutes, meditating. Then he got up, took a card out of his pocket, handed it to me, and made a motion telling me that I was dismissed. The card was in English and said his name, that he was 108 and the Buddhist patriarch of the region. It was the best moment of my China trip.

When I was with the great patriarch of Mexico, the same silence ensued. A polite silence ensued – one born of the difficulty of verbal communication. Respect lives in this silence. I finally tried to communicate with him; it was like we had never met. He made little effort to understand me, assuming I was another stupid gringo. *Was his dementia worse than I had thought?* Then Gloria came in and greeted him. I told her that I didn›t think he remembered me. So I got close to him and told him I was the guy who wanted to put solar electricity on his house.

Without missing a beat, he said, "Why didn't you do it?"

Gloria joined in, "That's why we are here, Tata Kachora. We just met with a solar engineer in Ensenada yesterday."

"Oh, I understand," he said, grasping that it was a big job.

So I say, "We were only gone for two weeks. We told you that we would return now."

He took this as an insult and a challenge, suggesting his memory wasn't good. "That was a month ago," he said.

Gloria jumped in to settle, agreeing with him. I later figured out that his 107-year-old memory was as good as mine. It had been exactly three weeks. I explained the whole thing again. He was now an environmentalist, as well as a great shaman. To complete the circle and help save Mother Earth, he needed to get his energy from the sun. He could then show the world *"Chingon,"* he said with his thumb up.

At this point, Marco entered and greeted Tata Kachora. A jovial conversation ensued between the two of them. He asked Grandfather if he really wanted me to write a book about him. While they were discussing something I couldn't understand, Grandfather jokingly asked him if I was a womanizer. They decided to play around and agree that I was. He suddenly looked stern, turned to me, and waved his finger.

"I don't want you writing a book about me."

Oh no, he was worried about getting burned by a womanizer. My partners suddenly realized the mistake and went into damage control mode. Gloria reassured him that I was a good guy. But he told her that I was using her youth to stay young. In actuality, she was 17 years younger than I. He used an old Spanish expression that didn't translate well. It described how a rooster stepped on the feet of a hen to hold her down. I was disappointed but not surprised. Experience has suggested to me that women are the Achilles heel of male shamans.

The moment passed, but I was not sure about things.

Presently, a tall, handsome man entered the room. He had a ponytail and was well dressed. Excusing himself, he squeezed by us to greet Tata Kachora and offered him a bag of shrimp. The two appeared close as they chatted. The man was called Thiago and shared that he was a local school principal. He turned out to be Tata Kachora's favorite student and financial advisor.

Thiago, who was upstanding, sober, and on the Red Path, had always been there for Tata Kachora. (The Red Path is the same one Castaneda called "The path with a heart." Tata Kachora considers this to be a metaphor for the Toltec philosophy.) As his most helpful and loyal student, Thiago reaches hundreds of eager children's minds through his job. Thiago and I had both realized that children would be the answer. They would have no choice! Thiago will someday be called "Tata Thiago". They may never call me Tata, but I'll tell you folks that my life had turned into one big, beautiful trip. I didn't need peyote. However, I will say that I got a lot further with *Mescalito* than many of Tata Kachora's students. I was a member of the Peyote Way Church. My friends there were excited to learn that Tata Kachora was still here, in this life.

Returning to the situation in the room, the others had all been ignoring a large young man with Thiago standing at the back of the room. I introduced myself to the fellow. He grinned self-consciously like a respectful child, singled out and spoken to by a visitor. He at first said that he was nobody. But was he really? The man was in the municipal police force of Tecate and was Tata Kachora's grandson. As I learned, he was a big part of Tata Kachora's security. One must understand that the King always has security surrounding him. The only difference was the informality. There are no Buckingham Palace guards, but people are always watching, protecting him.

Thiago stood up and motioned me outside. He then explained that Netflix had a contract with Tata Kachora; they were doing a documentary about him. I could not write about him or film him until the contract was up on March 22.

What now?

I felt confident that Netflix could never get inside this story in the way I could. My whole life had prepared me for this. But now I had to find out about the contract. Tata Kachora himself had even told us that someone had done a documentary on him. He had complained that they didn't get it right. They had asked about his famed knowledge of medicinal plants but failed to go into the fields.

So at this point, we had to ask: Were Americans so in love with the myth of Don Juan that they didn't want to know who the real guy was? Was it somehow less romantic? Not to me! I was thrilled to ask the real "Man of Knowledge" about the real Castaneda. But once you are inside his world, you learn to understand that it was just a chapter in one of the longest and most interesting lives anybody could be living.

Myth trumps reality! I was an iconoclast when it came to false idols. Damn fools. False idols should be broken. Tata Kachora was somebody I could see as a regular human, though he wasn't exactly regular.

Gloria was interested in his human side too. She asked if his teeth were real. This got him to tell us his stories. No, they had been knocked out in an accident. Long ago, he was riding a burro over a mountain. On the rocky ledge, the burro had stumbled, causing Tata Kachora to smash face-first into a rock, losing his front teeth.

Then he explained that he could remember a hundred

years of his personal history. Apparently, his earliest memories were from age seven. It seemed like his memories alone could fill a book.

"I like to explore and look for lost cities."

He said that he had seen the mounds of Cahokia, across from St. Louis, been to Maya cities, along with many ruins in between.

He talked about using his mind to remotely search for lost cities. I had read about this ability, but here he was actually telling us about it. There was a mention of an enchanted labyrinth somewhere as he tossed out many names and places.

I could relate because I loved to find Maya ruins that only some of the locals knew about. If you ventured into the jungles, you would discover them. The buildings were buried in vegetation and appeared to be little steep hills. It's after a while that you learn to spot them.

There were thousands of places whose names had been forgotten. Many of the bigger Maya cities had been partially evacuated. There was the huge city of Calakmul, buried deep into the jungle. Some were easy to reach, such as Hormiguero, Ant City, with its elegant homes, like Jaguar House. You enter the home through the mouth of a jaguar. Our luxury homes were nothing but ugly compared to a beautiful Maya home. Wonderful sculptures surrounded a central staircase. Inside, the homes were decorated with paintings, and each of them was a unique work of art in itself.

Each large city was a kingdom, surrounded by smaller cities whose leaders were forced into fealty, or alliance, with the King of the larger city. However, all those kingdoms eventually failed, just like our civilization is now doing. They failed because they became unsustainable.

"All we are is dust in the wind."

Tata Kachora understood all of this. And in a couple more weeks, he would have a shining example of sustainability: a solar array on his roof.

But was it all too late? Had we waited too long to listen to the visionaries, like my new friend Poncho? Were the fires burning in the woods and in our cars and homes destroying our lives? Ask the people from Paradise and Redding, CA, or from Talent, OR, who experienced the horror of fire. This was for real! And I felt it coming again! Where were the rains and the snow this winter? We elders here in rural California knew the fires would return this summer. The smoke would choke us again. Tata Kachora and the rest of us would once again have to survive the smoke. Yet, we were not adapting well enough to stop it.

I call myself an environmentalist. I have installed solar power on my little ranch in Mount Shasta. My thermostat is usually set in the 50s but the heater does use diesel. My Prius still gets 47 miles per gallon but it gets used often. All of these actions are a move towards sustainability, but even that is not enough…we will have to do much more . . . I have probably cut my energy use in half, but it isn't enough.

"Get small"

If you have money, do it now. You can continue taking steps to use less fossil fuel and replace it with renewable energy.

As Tata Kachora reminisces, I wished I could record because I was only catching parts of it. I didn't have permission yet.

On a recent trip to Italy, he told us of seeing little gnome-like people. To me, this was more amazing than the gnomes. There were trips to Germany, both future and past. After a big Solstice Dance in June, there was a trip to a conference of leading shamans, which was stunning.

We eventually felt like we had used up enough of his time and energy, so we excused ourselves. I was a little bewildered. He had scolded me and made it clear that he didn't want anybody who lacked character writing a book about him. Yet, I felt that we had gotten past that. The Red Path was my path again, and the book must continue.

Besides, he had 45 children and countless younger descendants. It was apparent that he had plenty of experience with multiple women. We were not as different as he may imagine.

The drive back to Ensenada was very scenic. Bright sun with puffy spring clouds hung above the Earth. The rains had come in January and February, just in time to turn the hills green. Flowers were starting to bloom. We passed small sleepy towns with quaint names like Rancho Viejo, where cows stood lazily chewing on grass. Then down through the wine route were perfect rows of grapevines and fancy wineries. One more hill to round, and there sparkled the shiny Pacific.

Things had started out innocently enough back in Ensenada. We returned to our room at El Rancho Motel. After a quick shower, Marco took us on a tourist spots tour. Gloria had never been to Baja, let alone its jewel, Ensenada. She loved the beach with the sunset over the ocean, eating shrimp for dinner, and being in Mexico.

Americans didn't appear to be part of the mix. Since COVID-19 hit, the Gringos were down to a few stragglers who lived in boats or had homes.

Things change so quickly when you're on a journey like

this. As I am writing this, I am alone at a high alpine lake. Ensenada is about 1000 miles south of here. My house is way down below in the valley.

It is May 31, and a stifling heatwave has already arrived. This might be my only chance to see the mountains and backpack before it dries out and the fires start again. It will also provide me with a chance to continue telling this story.

I hiked up here yesterday with Gloria, my brother, sister, and a nephew. They wanted to see the Caldwell Lakes where I was planning to camp, but they walked back in late afternoon, leaving here to camp alone.

The flowers are blooming, and the snow is almost all melted. There is a chorus of frogs chirping all around the lakeshore. Neon blue jays jump around pine branches as they scold me. There is no one here but the animals and me.

Now I can go back and try to make sense of what happened at the end of our last trip to see Tata Kachora.

On the way back from Mexico, Marco and I apparently began to stress out Gloria. She kept it to herself for a while. But she finally exploded on the way back to Yuma. She blurted out something about me wasting all my money. It was connected to the fact that I had bought Marco a new iPhone and was going to spend more money writing this book. Meanwhile, Gloria had to remain home working and taking care of our grandson, Leo.

Things were tense as the three of us drove back toward the desert. I wasn't sure what had really caused Gloria's outburst, but I guessed it had something to do with Marco.

Once we were alone and driving home from Arizona, tension was inside the car. I was avoiding dealing with her anger. But that somehow made me angry. When anger finally boiled over, communication failed.

She felt disrespected. But when she demanded that I compensate her more than Marco, I lost my temper. What had I done wrong?

My feelings were that she got to go on a paid vacation. I had even given her some cash to help compensate for lost wages. But we fought over money and respect. We broke up!

Now we are "friends." I've never really figured out what that means. But I guess it was like you don't hate each other.

However, I was still Leo's Grandpa. So we connected through him, even spending time with him in the mountains.

4

THE SPRING DANCE

Tata Kachora had invited us to the Spring Dance. I was feeling a little insecure as I drove alone into Baja for the first time in my life, because I no longer had Gloria by my side.

I didn't know how to get to the site of the Dance, so I drove to his house. No one was visible, so I waited. Pirate and Arrow remembered me and came up with their tails wagging. After petting them, I stood by my car, not wanting to be intrusive.

Eventually, his daughter, Irene, appeared in the doorway. I explained that I didn't know how to get to the site, and she said she would check with her father. A few minutes later, she came back and said I could follow him and his driver. But later, she returned and said he would not be going until tomorrow.

They had been polite, but I was feeling like an intruder. So I wound my way back down the hill to wait at the highway. I couldn't reach Marco on the phone. Was he even going to show up? Would I be considered an outsider if I made it to the Dance?

Negative thoughts begin to creep into your mind at times like this. I was alone away from home.

While I was waiting at a Pemex gas station, Marco called. He and his friend were almost there. Relief!

Most of the businesses near the gas station looked old and shabby. There were restaurants with handmade signs, little mom & pop stores, and a beat-up tire shop. The rows of businesses lining the highway were not necessarily old because about ten restaurants have been built along the highway to Pinacate over the past forty years (this is the part of Highway 2 where the criminals had been robbing everyone). Most of those restaurants rapidly crumbled to the ground. They are reduced to piles of rubble glistening in the desert. Only one is left. Businesses age quickly in rural Mexico.

Unsustainable development appears to be one of the biggest problems in Mexico. Oftentimes you will even see large new buildings abandoned because of poor planning. Well-meaning people had wasted their money by assuming people would come. Ruins are everywhere. The ground is damaged.

Sadly, Mexicali has that look. Coming from a place as beautiful as Mount Shasta, it is a striking contrast to drive through such a town. It just looks like rubble and trash with houses and, once in a while, a business mixed in.

Marco and his buddy arrive at the gas station, and I feel better. After buying some water and last-minute supplies at the local OXXO convenience store, Marco asks for directions to Canyon Manteca. This is where the Dance is being held. The road starts directly across the highway.

It's a bumpy dirt road that heads east along the base of a gray mountain. As I followed them, the road worsened. Big rocks stuck out, and the ruts got bad. It forced me to coax the Prius down that dusty road.

We were several miles in now. After the houses thinned out, we crested a pass to find ourselves looking down at a beautiful valley. The scene below was both timeless and awe-inspiring. Far below was a ring of dancers in Native American clothing, a sweat lodge, and a fire pit.

This was Tata Kachora's Sacred Site.

If it wasn't for the cars and tents dotting the ground near ancient oak trees, this could look like something that took place hundreds of years ago. I had never seen a more beautiful gathering.

It was high spring on the valley floor. The grass was short, and the whole valley was completely flat. We parked our vehicles next to a couple of huge live oaks. It was a good place to set up our tents because of the shade from the trees. My door was facing a mountain to the east, and no camps were blocking the view. The mountain was covered with bushes and small trees and had large granite outcroppings. There were other camps spread under the oaks. The whole valley had a warmth and sweetness in the air.

I wasn't ready to join the others, so I climbed partway up the mountain and smoked a joint. It was late afternoon, and I was tired when I got back to the valley floor. There was a giant oak tree that must have been a thousand years old. The middle of the tree was completely rotted, but there was plenty of strength in the wood left to stand strong during thunderstorms. Would it survive global warming?

Once the sun went behind the mountains, the March air grew chilly. I never left camp during the evening. I was tired.

There was frost on the grass in the morning, and everyone seemed to stay bundled up inside their tents. When the sun finally rose over the mountains, it warmed up quickly, and the whole camp came to life.

After having breakfast, I finally wandered over to the Dance area. The morning sweat was ending, and the participants were coming out of the lodge. They were steaming, and blinking in the morning sun. Most of the other campers were gathering too.

I was one of the people who stood out because I was the only tall, white American. There were also some Germans who were tall, blond, and very white. A young German couple arrived; they almost blinded us because they were wearing white clothes over their pale white skin. They brought to my mind a description I had heard before; white worms that had suddenly been exposed to the sunlight. They were arrogant when I spoke with them, telling me that they were flying him to Germany. Also, they told me they were the ones using his abilities correctly. They never asked who I was. They dominated the Dance that morning and became the color of lobsters from so much sun. Then, they jumped back into their fancy rental car and left after only half a day.

I can only imagine how intense the pain from the sunburn must have been. Everyone else at the Dance seemed to have Native American blood.

When most of the people had gathered in the morning sun, we said a group prayer. I was moved. Everyone was feeling the love.

People made sure I felt welcomed by smiling and making eye contact. A handsome man dressed as a Plains Indian dancer began organizing people for the morning

Dance. He asked me to get in line, but I tried to avoid dancing because I had just been on a hike. I told him I was too old, but he said he was in his sixties, too. I had no choice.

The Dance circle was marked off by two rows of white rocks that formed a big circle for the dancers. There were four more rows of rocks that led to a shrine in the center. The center shrine was an amazingly complex work of art that was basically a sculpture decorated with mosaics, paraphernalia, and other objects.

In the middle of the shrine was a live poplar tree, and leaning against it was a picture of a man about fifty years old. He was the son-in-law of Tata Kachora, who had recently died of COVID-19.

I was given instructions by the Dance leader. He was a tall businessman from Mexico City who had shared that he was also writing a book about Tata Kachora.

We dancers fell into line at the south end of the circle. Men were all placed between women because there were more women. Feeling a little self-conscious, I got in line. I was going to be noticed. My hair was long, and I had jewelry on. But more importantly, I was the only Gringo at the Dance.

Being a dancer was fun. The moves weren't too complicated, and the women next to me were always smiling and encouraging me. There was one young woman who really grabbed my attention. She was charismatic. Every time she danced past Tata Kachora, her energy was electric - sparks flew. She had the moves.

So we danced, and we danced, and we danced. We danced for the love we felt towards each other and for the love of the Earth, and for the love of Grandfather. As we danced past him, he was watching each one of us.

However, the Dance went on and on and on. I got tired and thirsty, and it became hard to keep up. Anybody could see that I was having a hard time. I literally had to put one foot in front of the next and force myself to continue. I started to feel that the guy leading the Dance was sadistic as he began correcting my movements. Were these dances supposed to last for hours?

When it finally ended, several of the dancers thanked me for "participating." The feeling of connecting with everyone and my surroundings returned. I had danced in front of my lifelong hero and received his blessings.

Tata Kachora had arrived just before the Dance started. Thiago had driven him to the site in his nice, black Ford truck. I was in the kitchen when he got out of the truck. I was stunned by what I saw. He got out and walked over to the kitchen - no cane, no helpers. This was after the long jarring ride from his house.

First of all, I had no idea he was still so strong. The other times when I saw him, he was at his house. He had never moved away from his spot, only appearing through his bedroom door or sitting in the chair.

It was a true revelation to see a man so in command of his body and mind at 107. He was well dressed, mostly in black. Under his fancy hat was his long white hair, tied back.

After he arrived in the kitchen, he sat down alone and held court for a while. People would walk over to his table, and he would graciously greet them and chat.

That was when the German couple drove up, jumped out of their car, and went straight up to him. They made a big show of greeting him and hugging him. Obviously, they felt special.

At one point, he recognized me sitting nearby. He motioned me over to say hi, asked how I was and told me to enjoy the Dance. We chatted for a bit, and I thanked him for inviting me to the Dance. I was flattered that he remembered me so well.

After a while, he got up and walked over to the ceremonial area. I followed behind, worrying that he would trip on a cow pie or gopher hole. He was slightly winded by the time he arrived.

Following ancient protocol, he went to the rock entrance at the North, said a blessing, and turned in a circle.

As he entered, several attendants came to him. A beautiful young woman held out the tobacco for him to carry to the fire. A young man with long braids came up with a jar of juniper embers and wafted smoke to him. (Juniper smells better than sage or incense).

His attendants scurried about him as if he were a medieval king. After finishing his entrance protocol, he sat on his throne: a plastic chair facing the dancers.

Just before the Dance had started, I was standing near Tata Kachora when a teenage girl came up and presented him with her baby. You could tell by his reaction that the baby was another of his descendants – another great-great-grandchild!

He greeted the girl with a big smile. Warmth flowed to the baby as he blessed her. It was a special moment.

After the Dance, I told my new friend Poncho about the girl with the baby and wondered out loud how many descendants he had. Since Poncho is a Mexican and an engineer, we decided to crunch the numbers and try to figure it out. We came up with a conservative estimate of at least a thousand. This was based on the fact that he had fathered forty-five children. Many of those children are now deceased or are in their seventies or eighties. Those people would have at least five or more kids on average, and so on. It is just basic demographics.

I told my sister about this, and she was critical of Tata Kachora. She said that it was not cool to have so many children and be proud of it.

Did she not understand that he was from a different time and culture? One that had almost been wiped out by non-Indians. His father was a Yaqui warrior who was among the last to fight Anglo-American oppression. The Mexican Government finally crushed the Yaqui resistance in 1926. They had to use modern bombers, artillery, and even armored vehicles for their success. The Yaqui men were mostly killed in the fighting. (see Yaqui History)

So, it was after the wars that a young Yaqui man grew up and took two wives. Tata Kachora says that his first marriages were sanctioned by the elders, partly because the tribe had few young men. They needed to increase their population.

The ethnocentrism of whites towards Native Americans continues to this day. My sister's position is an example. We middle-class whites do not realize how much white privilege we enjoy or how much we judge other cultures.

On some level, I am probably racist. And how many times have we heard an obvious racist claim not to be one? Look deep, people!

5

Spring Dance Ending

Tata Kachora is treated like a king by his followers. I have been around many famous people but have never seen someone treated like royalty. It is not surprising to see Tata Kachora's assistants instructing people about following protocol. He definitely has a regal air about him.

Tata Kachora arriving at his Spring Dance

After the Dance, I returned to my camp to eat and rest. A tall blonde woman arrived and began setting her camp near us. I had to pass by her. She smiled and said, *"Buenos dias,"* and I said, "Hello, neighbor," in Spanish.

She was having difficulty figuring out how to put up her tent, so I offered to help. We later became friends, as she spoke English and liked to smoke weed. Celeste was sweet. At first, I thought she was an American because she was tall and had blonde hair. But she later explained she was from Tijuana and had gone to school in San Diego. When my friends left later that day, she was the only person I knew besides Tata Kachora.

She would join me to hike partway up the mountain and smoke weed. We felt very comfortable together. She had two teenage boys in her camp babysitting her three-year-old when she was with me. I was happy to have such a friend.

Before Marco left, he had talked about trying to heal his friend, Alonzo, from trauma. He was trying to recover from a crisis that had almost killed him. Before COVID, he had been a healthy husband, father, and soccer player. Now he could barely walk.

Alonzo lives in Mexicali. He lives in the area where the houses are surrounded by trash and rubble. In that hellish place, he had contracted a bad case of COVID 19.

While he was sick, something even more horrible happened. Two of his kids were at a party and had gotten into a fight. The one on drugs had beaten the other to death with the crowd screaming for blood. In a rage of senseless violence, he had lost his beautiful daughter. People have told me that she was an angel.

So Alonzo laid in his bed, near death, with a gun to his head, trying to pull the trigger.

Marco was trying to keep him from killing himself. On the way to the Dance, they had stopped off at their Ceremonial Site in the high country. Marco instructed Alonzo to take mushrooms. He then told him to take off all his clothes and climb a hill. At the top was a huge granite boulder. Alonzo climbed to the top of the boulder. He laid his emaciated, white body down until the vultures began circling, thinking they would soon have a meal.

This is the way of a shaman, creating a symbolic death to purge the possibility of real death. Marco did the right thing. Alonzo said it was a good experience.

After telling me the story, they picked up their gear and left the Dance.

The battle against old age and death is the last battle a warrior must fight. This is right out of "the teachings." And this is the battle that Grandfather and I are now fighting. Death!

I should explain that as part of my research, I read *The Teachings of Don Juan* again. To become a "Man of Knowledge," one has to battle four enemies.

The first is "fear." At the end of the first book, Castaneda quits his apprenticeship because he is defeated by fear.

The second enemy is "power."

The third enemy you must conquer is "clarity."

And since the last enemy is "old age," it cannot be defeated. But you must fight as long as possible. And this is where Grandfather and I find ourselves.

Until I met Tata Kachora, I thought I would die sometime in my sixties. My thinking was that if I lived a large and exciting life, it would be better than just living as long as possible. Too many elderly people, my mother included, had suffered because they continued to be cared for when they no longer wanted to live. Ken Kesey and Hunter Thompson were my age when they died. But they had seen more than most people who live to be 100, and so have I.

I believed that I had lived such a wonderful and full life that I should quit using up resources and stop trying to hang on as long as possible. I was planning to join my cousin and so many others by using hard drugs to ease the pain. I would go to my sacred mountain and sleep. A gradual, painless death; it wouldn't be so scary that way.

"I'itoi, take me home."

Drugs are cheap down here. *Naked Lunch.*

Americans have bought into a myth that doesn't make sense. You are a slave to capitalism until you reach old age. If you manage to make it to the "golden years," you are now supposed to stop working and start "enjoying life." Even on the surface, the whole concept sounds wrong. How can the last years of life be the best time in your life? Really? Did you not enjoy your first sixty-five years when you were younger and healthier?

I have reached retirement age, and I'm glad that I only had one foot in that game. I feel compassion for those who did not enjoy their careers. They did the same thing for so long that it became their identity, whether they liked it or not. My father did not enjoy his career.

"Teacher" was my favorite career title, partly because it's almost impossible to make a living as an environmentalist. Technically, I do have a master's in secondary education and did teach in public schools. I use this title when convenient. Down here in Mexico, I try to avoid identifying myself because people happen to be more intuitive.

Do you think that Grandfather and I would be blessed to have had the lives we have if we had followed the American formula for a living? Hell no! Death is an advisor, and I listened all those years ago.

The mistake I made was to believe that I could live hard and fast – I would be all used up and have nowhere else to go. I was getting there when I met Grandfather and was reminded of the teachings.

You know, I am starting to feel like a real writer. Here I am holed up in a cheap hotel in Mexico. But I am rather enjoying the whole experience. My friends here in Ensenada are cool. The weather here is perfect, and you can actually afford to eat in restaurants if you are fairly poor. A writer!

Outside my hotel room, a party is raging in the streets. People must've piled in here from everywhere to escape the heat. It's so hot anywhere east of here that temperatures of 120°F were being recorded. I'm dodging it. My brother has been over in Yuma, Arizona, facing 116-119° F for the last few days. Global warming warning!!! Alert!!! Alert!!!

Everyone seems trapped but me. I don't get it.

After almost four days of dancing and celebrating, it was time to pack up and leave Tata Kachora's dance.

It seemed like a lot of the attendees were newly discovering their Native American roots. Thirty years ago, people here were mostly Catholic and traced their identity to Spanish roots. Things are changing.

Back then, I was teaching a class of fourth-graders, and we were starting a chapter on Native Americans. All of the kids were Mexican because it was in San Luis, Arizona. I asked the students what race they were, and they answered that they were "Spanish." Then I asked if any of them thought they were Native American. No one raised their hands. So I had to explain that the brown color of their skin was from Native American ancestors because people from Spain are primarily Caucasian. The kids were surprised but accepted this as fact because I was their teacher. However, they seemed to really enjoy the chapter once they realized their true roots were Native American. It was beautiful to see those cute little faces brighten as they realized their grandmother was using a grinding stone, just like the picture in the textbook.

Mine is one personal example of planting seeds of change in innocent minds. My subtle subversion was in the form of a teachable moment.

By the end of the Dance, I had made some new friends. People had made me feel very welcome, and I ended up spending time around the kitchen. This is usually the best place to socialize at large camping events. People really had a great experience that had something sacred at its core.

The whole four-day experience was one of celebration, spirituality, and community. With its grove of ancient oak trees and short grasses, the setting was perfect for the March Dance. It didn't get too cold or too hot. Even without Tata Kachora, it would have been special.

The drive out wasn't as scary as I had anticipated. There were dozens of obstacles, but you can get through an amazing amount with a front-wheel-drive car if you take them at the right angle. My car has a ground clearance of about four inches. If you do have to scrape the bottom a little, you just crawl!

As you start heading back, you begin passing the dusty gates of homes and ranches spread out at first. But as you continue, the ranches grow smaller, and the houses pop up more often. By the time you finally get back to the highway, you are basically in a town.

Now it was time to pull back on the highway and head south toward Ensenada and my next adventure. The "Wine Route" is no longer stressful to drive. It's pleasant driving over mountain passes and down into sleepy little places with romantic names like "Vallecitos." But once you truly hit the Wine Country, things turn upscale, and it reminds you of the California Wine Country. Many of the wineries have restaurants and hotels and look fun to stay at someday.

6
THE SUN SHAMAN

I arrived in Ensenada on time for my scheduled meeting with Poncho, the solar engineer. The sweet-looking guy had a ponytail with wavy graying hair. He dresses in shabby old clothes, and if you didn't know who he was, you would think he was poor. This is on purpose. He doesn't want to appear elitist, and it saves money.

Poncho is a real genius and a real leftist. He is one of the main solar pioneers of Mexico. And like I said before, he is a fan of Fritjof Capra.

We talked for hours about the paradigm shift that Capra told us we needed to create. We talk about Capra's ideas on sustainability and the conviction that we need to move towards an Earth-based spirituality. Capra gave the revolution a clear direction for the future and explained how the past led to the current crisis. His books are like bibles to us. *The Tao of Physics* wove together the new physics and the emerging Earth-based spirituality, and Capra's book *The Turning Point* is an inspiration and a roadmap to the future. His thinking represented the highest evolution of this school of thought that blossomed over the last seventy-five years. It started with writers like Aldous Huxley and Herman Hesse and led to guys like Poncho and me. The 1960's youth rebellion was a big part of the paradigm shift. However, these books and everything else failed to have enough impact. Our education systems have failed us. So now we have this fucked up world of humans destroying the real world. There just weren't enough people like Poncho. He is a friend living in the present, like me.

Poncho was born in Ensenada when it was a quiet, little town. When he was a little boy, his parents had a small store that catered to tourists. They sold sandals made from old tires, leather goods, ponchos, and the other usual assortments of tourist trinkets. The family of eight lived near the ocean, and Poncho and his friends roamed the hills and enjoyed nature.

As his parent's business became more successful, they saved enough money to put his two older brothers through college. Poncho was third in line, and his parents couldn't afford more schooling for him. But Poncho was an industrious kid who loved science. He even used to read encyclopedias when he got bored. I did that too.

So when he heard of a science contest sponsored by a large corporation, he entered a project. He won the grand prize, which was a scholarship to a university. His dream came true. In the end, he earned a master's degree in engineering. I like to call him a solar wizard because he was really a science whiz.

Incredibly, the two of us came from such different backgrounds, yet we ended up being so much alike. He even owns a small ranch in the mountains east of Ensenada. How amazing it was to find such a good friend down here!

He and his wife, Gaby, have created a sustainable ranch

that runs solely on solar electricity. He teaches classes in solar and has *cabañas* for rent. In many ways, it's similar to my place at Mount Shasta. It's also in the pines, and both ranches are in California (International boundaries aside). They were roughly the same distance from the ocean. His place is at a higher altitude, but mine is more alpine because it is 900 miles north.

I'm actually staying in one of his *cabañas*. He and his wife built everything here. Tourists come up here in the winter to rent *cabañas* and play in the snow. They come in the summer to escape the extreme heat in the big cities to the east. People even come to Rancho Puesta del Sol because they want to meet Poncho. Sometimes he entertains them by playing guitar and singing. He told me that last weekend some people came up to rent a *cabaña*, and we're extremely disappointed because he was in Ensenada.

This is one of those geographic areas called a sky island. The term describes high altitude areas where the plant and animal populations were cut off from other populations. At the end of the last Ice Age, temperatures increased, and living things migrated to higher altitudes and got separated from other populations. Now they live on sky islands. The animals cannot migrate any higher, so they are dying off. The deer, the coyotes, and even the pines are disappearing. Poncho is fighting a losing battle against the bark beetles.

Northern Baja is actually a high plateau. The altitude varies but averages about 5,000 ft. The highest part reaches above 10,000 ft. The areas with huge granite boulders are the prettiest.

The *cabaña* I stayed in was surrounded by them. There is a giant nest in between two of the boulders. It was made by a big wood rat. I noticed the pile of sticks while eating breakfast on a boulder in the first sunlight.

The morning sun rose on the frosty ranch. Poncho's wife, Gaby, was passing by with an egg she had just collected from a nest. She gave it to me and insisted I cook it for breakfast. It was still warm from the mother sitting on it. It was the freshest egg I have ever eaten.

Life on the ranch is all about demonstrating sustainability to visitors. Here, they live what they believe.

After two nights, it was time to return to Ensenada so we could go to Tata Kachora's house in the morning. Poncho needed to figure out the best place to install the solar panels. So we wound our way down the plateau to the west until we reached the semi-arid valley and town called Ojos Negros, or Dark Eyes. As the old ford chugged up the last costal range, we reached a pass covered with flowers. The sacred rains had been there!

On Monday, we took my Prius and headed to Tecate. Poncho had never been in a Prius, so he enjoyed the experience.

One last rainstorm had crossed some mountains on the way north. We noted the last burst of color from the wildflowers.

I pulled off the highway, where it summited a pass. The little dirt road was my new rest area because it provided a private view of the mountains and valleys. Drowsy little ranches dotted the distant valleys.

Poncho remembered the area from his childhood, "Look at this panorama. When I was a kid, there were many trees in the mountains. But with climate change and the fires, they are almost all gone."

It has been hard to see what has happened to Baja.

"...they are almost all gone."

"...almost all gone."

"...gone."

Sorry folks, we are two old men on a quest. But these fires will continue, so Poncho will keep fighting them.

Before we left, I prepared myself by going for a short hike and smoking. Then it was on to Grandfather's house. The world's oldest environmentalist would meet Baja's most influential environmentalist.

We got to the town and turned off the highway. We then wound our way up through smaller and smaller roads. We passed the little store, houses, and shacks until we reached the big house on Blue Mountain. When we arrived, I followed protocol by parking and waiting by the car. The front door was open as usual. After a few minutes, someone noticed us.

A woman greeted us from the top of the stairs. I told her we were putting solar panels up. Poncho explained that we needed to find the part of the property with the most sunlight. She told us we were free to work wherever we needed.

Poncho grabbed an old black case from the car. It contained the tool he needed to figure out where to place the solar panels. The device looks like a glass dome, resembling a giant crystal ball in a case. It was able to calculate the total sunlight reaching any spot. It was scientific wizardry.

As we were measuring the insolation, we rounded the corner of Tata Kachora's house and found him sitting under a tree, chatting with a student. I had seen the student before. He was in charge of the fire at the Spring Dance. His hair was short in the front but braided and long in the back.

As we walked over to them, Grandfather immediately recognized me. I was flattered as I greeted him. I introduced Poncho, who tried to say hello. But he waved Poncho off and asked me what Poncho was trying to say. Two months earlier, he had waved me off and asked Marco what I was saying. So I told Poncho to speak loudly and stand in front of him. Tata Kachora realized what I was telling Poncho. Then he said, "I'm getting deaf." It was surprising because he had never discussed anything to do with age-related problems. Poncho quickly figured it out. After that, they got along famously. Both are lovable guys.

A little while later, while they were talking, I decided to tell Tata Kachora that Poncho was a solar shaman. He seemed to love it and pointed towards the sun, saying, "A Sun Shaman. *Chingon!*" Then he pointed to himself and said, "I am a *nahaul*."

When he finished saying it, I was so excited that I blurted out, "And I am a nature shaman."

We were all in sync and laughing, and then Grandfather said, "Ok, you are an Earth Shaman."

What a moment that was for me. My heart soared like an eagle.

After a few minutes of getting to know Poncho, he got up so he could help us decide where to place the solar panels. He appeared comfortable, loose, and informal. We walked around listening to his ideas on where to place them. He suggested the roof of the big house. The cone-shaped roof, made out of stainless steel, would make it difficult. Also, the panels would have cut into the aesthetics. We talked him out of that idea.

Tata Kachora and Poncho the Sun Shaman

He was just a regular guy. I had never seen that side of him. At one point, he came out of his house, and his grandson, Ian, was playing in front. He chased Ian the same way I chased Leo, by almost running.

When a fight broke out between two dogs, Grandfather explained that a female was in heat. Then he joked that we men were like horny dogs, fighting over women. There is surely some truth to that!

He has that same personality I had known all my life, just older. Here he was, thriving, no cane, no feebleness, but you can really feel how ancient he is on another level.

It was a thrill to be hanging out with a guy I never even dreamed was still alive, let alone I could meet. It's like we were both reincarnated and are living in the future in 2021. How did we get here? This is not a dream!

In some ways, the Castaneda books have shaped my destiny – "The Path With a Heart," The peyote, and even realizing that I had taken "The Path." It may have been because of those old Castaneda books and this man.

After a while, we determined the only reasonable place for the panels was right on top of the small house. He agreed, and we told him we would be back in a few days to install the panels.

After we left, Poncho said it was an amazing experience. He had never seen somebody like Tata Kachora. Poncho also had an opinion on the Castaneda connection. "You can feel this man's power and importance . . . After you meet him, you realize that whether he was the guy from the books or not, it doesn't matter because he is a unique force."

I added, "Yeah, you can sure tell he's not your average asshole."

Poncho laughed for a while, then told me I was the only guy who would put it that way. Maybe.

7

THE INTERVIEW

Somewhere above the morning fog, a bright sun was rising. Below the fog, the light was still soft, and the air was cool and damp. The people of Ensenada wake up to a peaceful world.

The muted light was entering through many windows on top of the skeletal metal building. Two old men were stirring restlessly as they gradually regained wakefulness.

Poncho and I woke up in his building and quickly had coffee. We would have to skip the restaurant where we normally had breakfast. Poncho wouldn't be holding court at Poncho's this morning since we were too busy to spend half an hour placing our order.

It was a miracle that I slept at all because the day to do the solar installation at Tata Kachora's house had dawned.

His nephew arrived to load the truck at 8:00. Raul was a clean-cut college gymnast, hoping to make it to the Olympics. He was also Poncho's helper on that day.

Poncho's old truck was laden with equipment, and by that time, we headed north on the big highway that hugs the ocean. We saw an eagle, which Poncho quickly identified. He said that when he was young, those eagles did not live in the area. They had migrated north as the ocean warmed and the climate changed.

As we were heading up the Wine Route towards Tecate, my companions were hungry from loading the truck and driving. They wanted tacos from a particular taco stand, where they were made with *birria*. It is a Mexican delicacy made with goat meat. They were expensive for a poor Scotsman.

You can tell how much the standard of living in Mexico has gone up by the way most people consume beef. Forty years ago, it was too costly. Many people could only afford beans and tortillas. Cheap restaurants always had more emphasis on beans. Tortillas are still popular in Mexico, but half of them are made from white flour now.

There was a guy assembling some kind of large steel frame next to the taco stand. His little boy of around three was trying to help. I immediately sensed danger as this child was carrying pieces of angle iron around, thinking that he was helping his father. The ground was littered with metal to trip over. If one of those tiny fingers got caught between these pieces of steel, his hand could get smashed beyond recognition. But as we left, the child continued to play.

In the mountains we encountered that last green area with flowers again. It was well into April now. Wildflowers colored the hills and grew along the roadside. It was another burn scar where the flowers always come back first.

We arrived outside the "Magic City" (I'm not kidding, it's mentioned on the "Welcome to Tecate" sign) and wound our way up to Tata Kachora's house, arriving in the late morning. He came out to see what the commotion was all about and found Poncho getting ready to climb onto the roof.

I was just standing there, so he walked over to me and said, "Hi." He was alert and talkative. After a couple of minutes, he motioned me over to his "spot" on the wall, under the shade of an olive tree.

Note: I was allowed to record our conversation and take pictures on that day. There is also a photo included here. After all, I was installing the solar for free.

The following is part of a recorded, verbatim conversation between Tata Kachora and me. It reveals his great sense of humor.

"How many kids do you have?"

"I have 45 children."

"And how many grandchildren?"

When he answered, it sounded like he was saying '*cinquenta,*' or 50. But it was an old joke that I knew even though it was in Spanish.

"Fifty or more, huh?"

"*Eewi!* Yes, fifty like this, '*sin cuenta.*' Ha! Ha!"

"Oh, I get it."

"Yeah, yeah!"

"Without count, like the stars."

"Ah, hey."

"That's an old joke my father used to tell."

"Yes, the Highway of the Stars. *Chingon!*"

This is how well we communicate. I had the whole day to record, and I recorded as much as I could.

The Highway of the Stars is one of his mystical concepts. I was on it once when I took some acid. I got a long way into the stars, and I came to a white spiral staircase with three old men descending it. The guy in the middle had a bottle of whiskey in his hand and was very drunk. He looked at me, and surprisingly I realized it was me! I bolted up and out of the vision, yelling, "I just saw myself as an old man!" The message was obvious: Stop drinking!

As Tata Kachora was beginning to reminisce, I asked for his permission to record him. Instead of answering my question directly, he said, "Tata Kachora was born in Sonora," speaking of himself in the third person.

"The Yaquis were the original people. My grandfather was named Donaciano Aiguire and was related to a family with the last name of Gueremez."

What if everything that he says is true? We were back over a hundred years on the timeline of his amazing life. He begins interspersing Yaqui words that even Poncho can't recognize, so some of his monologues are hard to follow.

Next, I asked him about a picture of him working in a botanical store. The picture seems to be from the 1970s. That was around the time he had told Castaneda to get lost. He looks at the picture and nods.

"My grandparents opened a botanical store in 1919, and both of them attended the store."

Then he says that his grandparents came from a village called Emoris. The village was situated in traditional Yaqui lands in the Sonoran part of the Sierra Madre.

If he is correct about his time and place of birth, it was during the last Native American resistance to European domination. The Yaqui continued to fight for their freedom until the mid-1920s. As I mentioned before, they fought so valiantly that the Mexican government had to use modern bombers, artillery, and tanks to defeat them. They are legendary warriors (see Yaqui history in Wikipedia).

Tata Kachora has a picture in his house that was taken during that tragic era. I have seen the picture in history books, and it shows President Obregón with his generals and aides. One of them is a Yaqui named Luis Matus.

According to Tata Kachora, he was a descendant of Luis Matus, who was his grandfather. Matus was a general who was allied with Obregón during the civil war (see the old photo in the article mentioned above).

But in 1926, Matus fought against Obregón and captured him on a train. Somehow Obregón cut a deal and saved himself.

It is interesting to note that Castaneda gave Don Juan the last name of Matus. Was this another coincidence? (I also included a discussion of the historical and cultural significance of the name Don Juan at the end of this book.)

At one point, Luis Matus also fought on the side of Poncho Villa. Later, a man named Matus was killed by General Manzo. There is a lot more history to explore, but that is not the purpose of this writing, and I am not swearing to the accuracy of these accounts. I'm just trying to be as accurate as possible without too much research.

Tata Kachora believes two of his grandparents were deported or escaped from Yaqui territory by 1925.

He continues, "When I was older, my grandparents and I moved to Hermosillo. I lived in the desert near Hermosillo and worked as a lumberjack, cutting down mesquite trees to clear the land for planting.

I went to Caborca. I lived there and started a little botanical store to support myself. Later I moved to Tijuana."

"When was that?"

"Nineteen...forty...fifty, or forty-nine, I moved to Tijuana.

Tata Kachora around the time he rejected Castaneda

At that point, I said, "I thought you met Castaneda in Sonora?"

"Yes. Yeah, right. Another friend told Castaneda where to find me."

Then I asked him if he used psilocybin mushrooms, and he said "No." This tells us that the "Don Juan" who offered the mixture to Castaneda was a different person.

Then Tata Kachora told a story about giving Castaneda a different kind of mushroom.

Castaneda had asked Tata Kachora to travel to Oaxaca. There, Grandfather Shaman's friends had supplied Amanita muscaria mushrooms for Castaneda. "The red ones are the best. And because of this, my father called it 'The Red Path.'"

The Amanita muscaria has been used by shamans for thousands of years. They are the big red ones with white spots. But they are dangerous if you consume them without preparation.

I once experimented with them. My friend and I took them with no supervision. We did not know how to leach out the toxins, so the experience was not what it should have been. We vomited first. Then we had the feeling of being in a "sun storm." It was like being on an outdoor stage where the sunlight was blindingly bright, and an audience was watching. Strange!

He told me his version of what happened with Castaneda when he took "The red mushrooms . . ."

After all these years, the story had been distilled down to this: "I told the guys to tie him to a Sapote tree because he would try to jump and try to fly." This story sounds familiar. Maybe it was in a later book.

I just read Castaneda's description of his first experience with mushrooms, and it doesn't match Tata Kachora's version. First of all, Grandfather told me that he never used mushrooms. Why would he say that unless he was differentiating truth from fiction?

This is an instance of Castaneda giving Tata Kachora credit when it was about a different shaman, or he was making up the story from other stories he had heard. But we can see that Grandfather is being consistent because he told me the books were embellished with stories from elsewhere. He clearly knows which parts are true. Those first mushrooms Castaneda took were not given to him by Tata Kachora. Period. The latter story is probably true because I heard it from Tata Kachora himself.

The Red Path philosophy comes from his father and appears to originate in Southern Mexico. "My father passed me the concept of The Red Path. He said, 'This will always be the name of the path because this is where our brothers and sisters from India emigrated from. They brought the *footprints of wisdom*, and this spread all over Mexico and the world. It is written in the history books. This is a very long story."

At that point, he paused, so I interjected, "You, yourself, have a long history."

"How was Tata Kachora initiated?" He said as if he was asking himself. "The teachings of my father and my mother. I had to learn and learn and learn about the plants. I was learning about all the plants until we got up to 10,000."

Then he changed the subject and said, "People ask me, 'Shall we write a book?' Only if you follow me on 'The Red Path.' You.

"I want a plant book, and the pictures have to be in color or no deal – big books with pictures in color. It could be 1,500 pages. Of my personal history, the book will be three or four hundred pages. I've been writing my story up till now. If it gets to three or four hundred pages, it will be a good book.

"This thick."

He held his fingertips apart to demonstrate the thickness.

His daughter appeared with a batch of freshly made sage wraps and set them in the sun to dry. When I walked over and picked one up, he said, "Don't touch them! They are not ready." According to him, he had made them. Good enough for me. After they had dried, I bought three. Next time I attend a drum circle in Mount Shasta, I will light one.

We both agree that in order to capture most of the important information on his life, it would require three books. This book reveals the real person behind the Castaneda books. Another book should focus on his plant knowledge, and the third should focus on his personal history.

Continuing with the conversation: "The book will be a bestseller because Tata Kachora is in it."

"Do you realize that the Americans think you have been dead for 40 years?"

He answered, "No. These are the names of all my children."

"But the Americans think you're dead."

"No. On my path, there is much envy and greed."

"There are Americans who had found me . . . when I was young with my parents, in the mountains. And walking and learning about the plants."

"Now they have people called homeopathic doctors. They have botanical stores now. I trained students in the knowledge of plants while we were hiking. I told my students, 'You are not a medical doctor. You are a homeopath or a *curandero* because you use natural medicines.'"

Suddenly he interrupted himself. "Hey, Sweetie, don't throw the water away. Come here and stop throwing away that dirty water." His daughter Irene and a granddaughter were trying to deal with a sewage problem. He kept yelling, but they ignored him. Finally, his granddaughter came over and stood in front of him, yelling as she explained the problem. I reflected again on the number of children and the estimated number of grandchildren he has had, thinking he may have broken some kind of record there.

Then he began talking about his favorite subject: His wives. "I found my fifth wife. She is here now." He even joked that she had worn him out the night before. Unbelievable, but I was there. Later, I heard a story confirming his prowess from someone who knew from experience.

I had known about his new wife since our last visit. She was at his house and was the same young woman from the Dance – the one whose moves were electric whenever she passed Tata Kachora.

When I saw her at his house, she said, "Hi" to me. I asked her if she was one of his daughters-in-law. She said without hesitation, "I am wife number five," as she held up her hand, palm open, signifying the number.

Stunning! She looked to be around thirty and very dynamic as well as attractive. She had very angular or pointed features yet appeared Native American. This was not surprising to me because there is a tribe in the Sierra Madre called the Tepehuanos, and they are tall and slender. They do not have features like most Native Americans, but they have black hair and dark skin. This amazing woman had a similar look.

I accidentally made a haunting video of her with my iPhone. In it, she appears and disappears while she is walking past Tata Kachora's house, just like a ghost that fades in and out of our vision. When I first saw it,

I wondered, *how did this happen?* But seconds later, I recognized it as one of the dozens of mystical ways I accidentally discover and create things. I soon took it as a sign that her presence in his life would not last long. How long can that marriage last?

I couldn't help remembering what Tata Kachora had told Gloria about me. He said that I was using her youthful energy to stay young, almost sucking it out of her. I am 17 years older than she is. He is about 80 years older than his new wife. Gloria and I broke up a few days after this. I am just pointing out a few facts here.

So with this subject, we have entered politics because it does affect the world of shamans. I have observed that jealousy and hypocrisy are problems for several of us. We should not single out Tata Kachora. For example, his peers have provided me with a picture of the last thirty years of his life, but their perspectives may be colored by jealousy. Our egos do get in the way and change our perspectives on past events. This has been the hardest part of my experience with them. The results have made me isolated from Tata Kachora.

In recent years as Tata Kachora's fame has grown, the other shamans around him have watched him enviously. He has developed a group of followers (students who are now in their thirties) who assist him. These students are close to some of his younger family members, but they have alienated the shamans from my generation, including me. In conversations, I've discovered how the older ones believe Tata Kachora's popularity is largely based on his claim that he was Castaneda's teacher. Some also pointed out that they helped him a lot and were not appreciated. Some aren't even convinced that Tata Kachora was the person Castaneda used as the model for Don Juan.

Is there jealousy involved? Of course, we are talking about human nature. My generation of shamans has watched Tata Kachora grow in fame and stature. They have worked hard to create an alternative worship Site. So they feel somewhat cheated because their contributions helped Tata Kachora and the younger group, and they didn't even get credit. One example is the Spring Dance. Oso learned it from the Lakota Sioux and taught it to Tata Kachora.

The site that Tata Oso and the others have created serves as an alternative to the one used by Tata Kachora and the young people. It is prettier and can be visited at any time. There is also a more viable community connected to the site. Oso is even selling land to people who want to own land there. The area looks similar to the most beautiful parts of Southern California. I have promised to provide the site with solar electricity since it is off-grid.

The Elders of this community sat down with me and explained that Tata Kachora is cashing in on his newfound fame because he has only been saying that he is the guy from the books for about ten years. And furthermore, a couple were reluctant to agree that Castaneda and Tata Kachora knew each other at all. But it was not important for them to get the facts right, so emotions color their opinions. Also, they didn't meet him until years after the Castaneda period. He didn't have a reason to bring up painful memories with them. He had succeeded in moving on.

Tata Kachora's ex-girlfriend was part of the conversation. Her daughter was listening and started doing some research for me. She quickly came up with evidence that proved Tata Kachora and Castaneda knew each other. Her mother was reluctant to agree. (She found a fragment in the book, *The secret life of Carlos Castaneda*.)

There are always differing opinions in any community. It is human nature. As we see, this community has deep divisions. However, I have seen Tata Kachora and Tata Oso talking on their cell phones several times. They love each other.

It is also interesting to note that Tata Kachora and other old shamans in this community dress like aging rock stars. Keith Richards, Tata Kachora, Mapuche (To be discussed later), and I often wear multiple necklaces and bracelets. For the Old Man to be over 100 years old and look so cool is somehow comforting and heartwarming.

On a serious note: the message from all my shaman friends and me is the same. Connect your identity to the Earth and help us save it! Everything is connected!

8

Don Fyo: Maya Shaman

This story would be incomplete if I didn't explain how this whole journey began. It began with a fantasy long before I met Tata Kachora. Ever since the Zapatista Revolution surfaced in 1994, I had wanted to visit the State of Chiapas. It is arguably the wildest part of Mexico. I wanted to meet the rebels, and a real Maya shaman. The Earth was kind and provided me with somebody that was both. Thus, this chapter is about how it really all began:

Gloria and I are in the state of Chiapas, Mexico. We are walking in the jungle at night, being careful not to trip. Out of the nearby blackness comes a deafening roar. Instead of running back to the *cabaña*, we calmly continue walking toward Felicia's little outdoor restaurant. We are conditioned and now know the sound. Our senses have gotten used to the deafening roars in the jungle night. It's only the big howler monkeys. They are part of this ecosystem. It is late December, and we are here with the Maya, the pyramids of Palenque, the mountains, and the monkeys. No longer tourists, we are part of the mix.

Palenque is the jewel of all the ancient Maya cities. For years I had wanted to see it as part of a pilgrimage into the wilds of Chiapas. Gloria and I set out in November 2017, and it was wild, and it truly became a pilgrimage!

Now we are back here again and comfortably nestled into our usual *cabaña*. We feel so connected to this place. This trip is different because my adult children are joining us. I wanted them to experience my new home. It is also the home of Don Fyo, the shaman of the Global Revolution, the Zapatista fighters, and the howler monkeys.

The extremes of yin and yang are visible here in everyday life. You see blood on the hands of a woman as she merrily cleans a chicken. You find yourself in a crowd gathered to watch a man die in the street, run over by his ex-lover! The hospital was a block and a half away, and the ambulance didn't push through the crowd. They just sat in it while the man lay dying in the street. I had to push my way through the crowd of onlookers to escape the tragedy. (Gloria's teenage brother died the same way as this man in Palenque, killed because he was on the motorcycle with his targeted older brother.)

Chiapas, Mexico – A world where life and death do not seem far apart. Yin and yang. It is not the world of middle-class Californians. And so my progeny will join us because this world is the real world. There is no sprawling suburbia to insulate them from it.

The thought fills me with joy and anticipation!

As we wait for them, we hang out in El Panchan. Panchan is a little enclave of restaurants, *cabañas,* and freedom. It is a space apart from the restrictions of normalcy.

The tourists here are not "normal tourists." This is the underground of tourism. They are the alternative to the occasional groups of typical middle-aged American tourists who find their way here. They are dentists from Michigan, psychologists from New York – white worms again. They come to see the ancient city of Palenque but look out of place in Panchan. The locals are mostly Maya or Latino. The outside rules do not apply in Panchan.

Mushrooms and marijuana are a big part of the magic. People trade medicine of all kinds without paranoia. In the evening, customers often eat while they slide comfortably down from a psychedelic high into a beer and weed euphoria, then stumble happily down one of the paved sidewalks to where they sleep, eventually dreaming of monkeys and toucans.

I never saw anybody lose control or destroy the ambiance at Felicia's. Even the local hustlers sometimes get drunk and mumble harmlessly in the background. It is a sacred place, like hot springs or a drum circle.

One of the locals shared that off-duty cops frequent the restaurant. They show up in plain clothes, smoking, and drinking like other customers. In Mexico, places can be exempt from the regular laws. This usually depends on local culture and how much money is involved.

On our first trip, we arrived as wide-eyed tourists. A young French couple told us to stay in El Panchan, at the *cabañas* called Jungle Palace. Jungle Palace is a collection of funky *cabañas* spread along both sides of a creek. A beautiful arching footbridge connects them. The workers manicure the jungle. It is so beautiful and peaceful. Our favorite *cabaña* has a porch over the creek. The clear pool below has little fish that I feed with tortilla crumbs. They all jump and fight for the crumbs.

Giant vines with huge leaves form spirals up the tall trees where the monkeys reside. Sometimes the giant castañuelas pods fall from trees and miss you by a few feet. They are edible. Once in a while, the monkeys get into a howling match overhead, and the sounds are deafening. You can leave, wait them out, or maybe yell back at them. But nobody yells back.

The guests at Jungle Palace usually come for the mushrooms and marijuana. But they are also there to see the great and ancient city. Palenque is often considered to be a Maya masterpiece. We who are lucky enough to discover El Panchan also find ourselves a few hundred yards from the arch that marks the entrance to Palenque National Park (Parque Nacional de Palenque.)

The city contains the pyramid of the famous "Red Queen," the splendid central palace, and many temples. Each temple was erected by a different king. During the peak of its power, the city was once adorned with sculptures paintings and plumes. It was 100 times more beautiful than one of our modern cities. We are so naive to think that our cities are worthy of comparison. It was also the last city to fail. Having finally defeated the other nearby city-states, it stood alone in its splendor. Which of our great cities will be the last to fail?

Our adopted home, El Panchan, is a little over a mile from the ancient city center. If you explore the jungle around Panchan on foot, you realize that it was once a suburb of the old city. Buildings are still buried in the jungle-covered with 800 years of growth. A farmer once encountered me on a trail and invited me up to his farm to see its Maya buildings. They were covered with vegetation and looked more like little hills than buildings.

My first little adventure in Panchan was sweet enough to share. We had found our way to Jungle Palace and settled into the *cabaña*. We soon ventured out to explore the surroundings. The curving sidewalk joins the little arched wooden bridge that leads over the sparkling water. The vegetation is partially cleared, leaving only beautiful, exotic plants with long stalks of flowers. There are also tall trees along the way. Giant rodents called *cereques* scurry through the undergrowth. They look like huge, fat squirrels with the back legs of a rabbit and square heads.

We wandered the short distance to the few bars and restaurants upon leaving Jungle Palace. We arrived at a small, white building that served as a beer bar. The bartender stood outside the building, surrounded by a chest-high bar that went around on one side. He occasionally entered through the door to retrieve a big bottle of beer called a *cawama*. An assortment of interesting characters was drinking beer in small groups around a sort of courtyard. Sensing that this was the place to score, we approached the counter and ordered a *cawama*.

A few moments later, a guy came up and offered to sell me some mushrooms. His name was David, and he looked like a large elf. His twinkling gray eyes are mesmerizing. We liked each other, and after haggling for a few minutes, we made a transaction. While we were getting to know each other over beer and joints, I inquired about hiking in the jungle. He invited me to join him for a hike the next day.

We got up in the morning to join the tourists and explore the ancient city of Palenque. After reading countless articles, I was finally in the greatest Maya city of all. It was deeply moving!

After returning to Panchan and having lunch, I went to see if David was around. He was easy to find and said he was ready to take me hiking. I joined him as he led me through the small labyrinth of Panchan and onto a rocky dirt road. In the jungle, we came to a sunny clearing filled with butterflies. Some were huge and flashed electric blue wings. The road led to the main road in a few hundred yards, but it was after the Park entrance with its giant arch. David told me that nobody cared if you snuck in and hailed a *colectivo*, a collective taxi. That way, it only costs 20 pesos to get in.

We walked along the road, passing plants with giant leaves. David pointed out toucans in the trees. It was late afternoon as the tour buses passed us on the way out. About a half-mile down, we turned onto a path that led uphill into the jungle. The canopy closed in overhead. There was a commotion as we startled a group of monkeys. They quickly scurried off through the trees.

After about ten minutes, we arrived at a small creek where the rock was all white limestone. He proudly led me across the creek and up to a waterfall. A fifteen-foot monkey face made of limestone stuck out of the falling water. It was perfect for a guy wanting to escape from the coming disaster back home. Trump had just won the election, and I was deeply concerned about America's direction. No Trump here!

Then David bathed in a pool while I sat nearby. When he returned and sat next to me, he opened his backpack. Magic and shamanic energy began swirling as he took out the contents. He filled a large stone pipe with layers of substances as I watched. First, a layer of weed, then a layer of something that looked like white sage, followed by another layer, etc. Before taking a hit, he offered me one. Naturally, I inquired about the contents I couldn't recognize. He told me that it was his blend of *ayahuasca,* weed, and other substances. I was very tempted but decided not to try it because I was 63 years old and had health issues. Big mistake! I should have done it.

So I watched as he took a hit. Then he sailed away on some unseen wind, deep into a state of complete grace and oneness. Rising to his feet, he stumbled a few yards. I could see that David had connected directly to the source of all life. He stood, rapture swirling around him, raised his arms, and slurred the words, "Pacha Mama!"

Mother Earth! His mother was holding him close to her womb.

In Carlos Castaneda's books, he and Tata Kachora never reached this level in all their time together. Tata Kachora was right. Castaneda wasn't there! But David is, and in a sense, so am I. Because I have fifty years of experience, education and history on my side.

Back on Earth, David returned to my side after about a minute and sat down. The medicine was already wearing off. He took another hit, but he remained sitting next to me this time, silently swaying back and forth. Suddenly, two young, innocent-looking German tourists appeared, so I greeted them. David's head was bowed, and he didn't want to acknowledge their presence. They looked bewildered, like people who had suddenly stumbled onto a couple having sex. I felt some explanation was in order, so I mumbled something about *ayahuasca*. They stood dumbfounded until David spoke in Spanish, "I only want to hear the monkeys and the wind." The Germans had been dismissed. Upon the realization, they left immediately.

David quickly returned to a normal state. The whole experience seemed to last only about five or ten minutes. My new friend had taken a trip to the heart of the Earth and returned. That's fast!

We began talking again. Realizing that I had lost track of time and it would soon be black as a jungle night, I suggested that we better start heading back. We didn't have a light, and there were many roots and stones to trip over. He quickly packed his backpack, and we started walking back.

After about 50 yards, I stumbled a little bit. He stopped and told me that I needed something to help me see in the dark. Quickly opening his backpack, he took out a woven basket with a red handkerchief covering its contents. There was enough light to see that it was filled with mushrooms of many sizes. (I had assumed that all psilocybin mushrooms were the same but later learned that they vary, and guys like David know the difference.) He handed me one and said it would allow me to walk in the dark. I trusted this fellow shaman and ate it immediately. I was all in! We were with Pacha Mama, and I had faith in her. I almost immediately felt a lift as she began guiding me in some mystical way. No more stumbling. Only beauty!

Gloria was waiting to eat dinner when I returned, and I was getting hungry. She had been worrying about me. I had found a new home in the Maya jungle!

In the morning, we took a *colectivo* into the modern city of Palenque to shop. It is about six miles from Old Palenque. Most of the people there were Indigenous. There are many tribes in Chiapas besides the Maya. The women wear traditional dresses only worn by women from their specific tribe. Hence, their tribal identity is apparent to anyone who knows them.

We felt ready to see someplace outside of the Palenque area by the fourth day. Before leaving California, I thought that maybe we could meet a Maya shaman. I met some "medicine men" in my youth when my family lived on the Navajo Reservation. But that was many years ago.

So, Gloria and I talked it over and decided to see if any locals knew a shaman.

We walked over to the beer bar and sat down near David and other local guys. They talked about a poor monkey who had fallen out of a tall tree and hit the concrete next to them. I asked what happened to the monkey after it hit. They told me that, after a minute, it had slowly gotten up and wandered away. It was possible to be severely injured between the falling monkeys and the falling castañuela pods.

After discussing the poor monkey, Gloria and I inquired if anybody knew an old Maya shaman in the area. One guy volunteered that he knew a very old and wise one. He would charge us $400 pesos for a day trip to meet him. The old man was an expert on mushrooms, and his ranch was a good place to take them.

The young man was named Luis, and we had no way of knowing where he was leading us. He promised that his shaman friend was very old and interesting. So we quickly got ready. I put my jar of mushrooms and honey in my backpack. We also invited a young couple to join us. They were eager for an adventure and had scored mushrooms for themselves. The guy was a handsome and sexy Italian, and the woman was a young, fashionable Mexican from Veracruz. Their romantic energy was as steamy-hot as the air.

Luis drove us in an easterly direction. We passed the

town of Roberto Barrios. It is known for two reasons. The first is its series of spectacular waterfalls, and the second is its strong Zapatista Government. They are rebels, and you can feel it. We did when we visited the waterfall on the previous day.

We had arrived in the parking area and were accosted by a group of children who offered to "protect" the car. I had long ago learned that you have to pay them in these situations because you are actually protecting the car from them. If you don't pay, you will return to a damaged car. While we were at the waterfalls, a young German tourist began running around, yelling that someone had stolen his backpack. We clung to our belongings, nervously eyeing the kids.

The waterfalls were a beautiful aquamarine and had many dramatic drops lasting about a quarter-mile. I made a beautiful video of Gloria sitting below one. Roberto Barrios is worth seeing if you are careful and willing to pay "protection money."

Upon returning to the rental car, we were met by the same group of kids. Having no idea that I was not a typical "white worm," they again demanded money. This pissed me off, and I looked at them with fire in my eyes.

"Gloria, can you stay out and keep them away from the car?"

"I paid you already, and you are making me mad!"

Listening to me yell at them in Spanish, they realized we were not the people to attack. Carefully monitoring their proximity to the car and with Gloria outside, I backed out. They wandered off, and the situation was over. The boys were right to back off because I would have gone to the Elders. I would have told them that I support the Zapatistas.

That was the main purpose of my trip. (It secretly, really was.)

Such was tourism in areas controlled by them. As we drove through their strongholds like San Cristóbal de las Casas, I had already made donations. But one size doesn't fit all when it comes to Gringos.

So we drove on, past villages with brightly painted houses, banana trees growing everywhere, stray dogs lying in the dirt, and past men and women who were scarred from battle who wore their scars proudly. We were not in Kansas anymore.

The highway started to angle up the lower slopes of some mountains, and the jungle grew dense. On the way, we chatted with Luis. He had a classic Maya look, standing about five feet, five inches tall, with black hair and a slightly rounded face and body. He was fairly good-looking and was a good driver. However, his responses sometimes seemed elusive or contradictory when we asked him questions. Overall, he was pleasant.

A few miles later, we approached a bridge when Luis suddenly hit the brakes and turned left. He stopped in an open, level area below the highway but far enough away to be insulated by a layer of the jungle. It was lovely, with grass and a few thatched huts.

As we parked, a man my age came walking towards the car. He had short, graying hair and wore a baseball cap, a blue T-shirt, jeans, and tennis shoes.

Luis said, "That's him." There was an obvious disappointment from the others, who must have been expecting to see a man in long, white robes, etc. But I had no expectations. And seeing him dressed casually at his home didn't bother me. Luis introduced him as Don Fyo.

He seemed warm and genuine as he invited the group to enjoy swimming in his river and hiking.

The others did not appear as curious about Don Fyo and quickly headed towards the river. I stayed with him and accepted a tour of his shamanic shrines. He also showed me several medicinal plants. We quickly hit it off. There was an immediate bond forming.

As he guided me towards the river, he asked how old I was. Before telling him my age, I mentioned that I had just asked Luis his age, and he had refused, saying it was rude to ask a Maya his age. Fyo scoffed at this, saying that Luis was full of it. I told Fyo that I was sixty-three, and he smiled pleasantly. "We are the same age. Maya emphasizes numbers, and this is a good omen."

He suggested that we might want to chat more after I returned from the river. I asked him for advice on taking mushrooms at his river, and he volunteered that he had never taken them. Luis had made up that part, too. I laughed upon realizing that I was the real mushroom shaman. Fyo agreed and also started laughing. The idea that he could serve as my guide became hilarious. He led me to a sacred spring, where I filled my water bottle, and we parted ways. I'm sure he had work to do.

The river was beyond beautiful. It had waterfalls entering from the side every hundred yards or so. The Karst topography (limestone) created a mystical world of water and rock.

The mushrooms began to take effect almost immediately, and the disorientation that often begins a psychedelic trip began setting in. Worse, my body wasn't prepared for the oppressive noontime heat. I realized that water was my only option. Practically tearing off my clothes, I grabbed a vine for balance while staggering down the steep bank and into the clear water. But the water was colder than I'd expected, and the bottom was rocky and bothered my feet. So I was still feeling insecure and uncomfortable. The water was too cold, and the air was too hot. I was fretting and freaking a little. I began yelling for Gloria to come and help me. She was not high and was somewhere nearby talking to Luis.

When she finally showed up, I explained how I was feeling. She looked annoyed but brought me my boots anyway. I took her to look to mean, "You got yourself into this . . ." No nurturing for me!

But the water had cooled me off and solved the physical problem. I just had to balance my mental side. Climbing the steep riverbank forced me to look up. I noticed a group of monkeys sleeping in the trees above. They were smart enough to sleep through the noontime heat. The secret was to stay cool! Lesson learned. I put my shirt on wet. It wasn't uncomfortable because the humidity kept it a little cooler than the air. Now my trip could start without worrying about a heat stroke or other physical problems.

I found Gloria and Luis resting in the shade of the monkey trees. The mushrooms had come on so fast that I was already peaking. It was going to be a short, fast trip. Let's go! Time to smoke some weed and cut the edge with a fourth of a zany bar.

The beautiful river became mesmerizing. It pulled me back down, and I began looking for a place to sit. Then I found my shaman throne! A large boulder was the right shape for a chair and had nice, thick moss for padding. Perfect! I always need to find the right spot to sit and meditate with psychedelics. It has become a ritual.

My throne was directly across from the most amazing waterfall. It dropped thirty feet from the opposite bank. Since it was limestone, the white rock had reformed in the waterfall and created sculptures of all kinds. There was an amazing pool halfway down. The water was contained by a natural, curved wall about fifteen feet long. The other side of the pool ended somewhere in the blackness of a cave that went into the waterfall. The idea of swimming in the pool entered my mind, but it made me shudder when I looked into the blackness of the cave.

Meanwhile, I had no awareness that Luis was starting to romance Gloria. So when I returned and found them chatting, I sat down. It was afternoon now, and the heat was diminishing. While they talked, I lay on my back watching the primates above. They were waking up and starting to move through the trees. They swung on vines and moved gracefully. The alpha males develop big jowls and look ugly to most humans. But the smaller ones are cute and conform to our image of a "normal" monkey.

At times, I entered the conversation with Gloria and Luis. He again underestimated my bullshit detector and fed me some false information. At that point, I felt it necessary to explain to him that he was not fooling me but rather irritating me. I also told him that if he wanted to succeed in the underground, it required honesty. It was dangerous to be dishonest. He wasn't listening.

After coming down a little, I decided to hike back and visit with Don Fyo. He suddenly seemed more interesting than the jungle itself. After all, he and the jungle and its medicine are all one. The walk along the river trail was filled with mystery and beauty.

One of the electric blue butterflies appeared, flying back and forth on a sunny section of the trail. I stood still and watched it fly around me. The blue flashes and the trails that followed were a show to behold. Giant vines climbed the big trees with their huge leaves spiraling upward. *Pacha Mama, you are everything!*

Emerging from the jungle at dusk, I found Don Fyo under a ramada. He got up and walked toward me, smiling.

"Did you enjoy your time at the river?"

"Yes. It is the most beautiful river I have ever seen. I also like your caves."

"Yes, the one with the mummy is named 'Tits.'"

We sat at the tables and got to know each other better. We were alike in many ways. He said there were some things he wanted to ask me about but did not know what questions were acceptable in my culture. I said I felt the exact same way. So we agreed that nothing was off-limits. What an opportunity for learning.

Mushrooms or no mushrooms, you remember almost every detail of an encounter like that.

He began by asking me about politics. What did I think of Trump? All present at the table agreed that Trump was the Antichrist. I said that the United States was in trouble and Trump was evil. Then Fyo asked about Mexican politics. I knew a fair amount. Institutional Revolutionary Party (PRI) is the corrupt party that almost always wins national elections. They're the rich people who endorse crooked politicians that win rigged elections.

They are the evil that the Zapatistas attacked on January 1, 1994. During the beginning of the Civil War, the Zapatistas briefly took over several cities and seized control of rural areas. The Indigenous rebels were led by a charismatic "spokesman" who went by the title

"Subcomandante Marcos." Looking every bit like Che Guevara: he rode a horse, carried a sawed-off shotgun, and had ammo belts slung over his shoulders. The Zapatista leaders like Marcos had ideas based on the writing of Karl Marx but were not interested in becoming another Cuba. Marcos did not want the Revolution to turn into a "cult of personality," where the leader becomes more of a dictator.

The Zapatistas and their Revolution were never defeated, but they were forced underground after the initial battles. PRI and the Mexican Army had unlimited resources, so the Zapatistas had to give up direct control of the larger cities. But they remain, both politically and physically, active to this day, controlling villages like Roberto Barrios.

I have read a book about the Zapatistas, and I support their Revolution. I even look a little like Marcos, and our names sound similar. He is a hero of mine.

And now I was sitting with real Zapatistas. They were soldiers who had seen their friends die in the struggle. Real revolutionaries who shared that the war had actually cost around five thousand lives! My brother was a TV reporter who was sent to Chiapas to cover the story of the Zapatista attack. The initial government statements put the death toll at less than a hundred, so my brother and the other media representatives were misled. Several Zapatistas told me that the real number of fatalities was grossly underreported because PRI lied to the media.

At that point, Gloria announced that she was cold and went to sit in the car. Luis followed her, suggesting that they should hold hands to keep her warm.

By now, Fyo and I were locked deeply into a meeting of the minds. We saw each other as equals. He told me that his sons were also shamans. They were standing in the twilight nearby, waiting to be introduced.

First, he introduced Raul. Raul told me that he sang to the Pacha Mama. He was a handsome guy in his mid-thirties. He politely asked me if I wanted him to sing. I agreed, and he sang. It was a love song to the Earth, beautiful and haunting. I was standing directly in front of him.

It was getting intense. I was now alone with a group of men who had known each other for a lifetime. But Fyo did not let me feel like an outsider. He and the others treated me like a fellow revolutionary. He supplied beer and allowed me to smoke weed. The drugs allowed me to feel comfortable and be myself.

Next, Fyo introduced me to his son Miguel, who was a warrior shaman. Miguel was huge and powerful, being the biggest Maya around. We shook hands. I laughed and grabbed his muscles, telling him I had never met such a powerful warrior. He giggled while his father stood proudly smiling. I was much taller than Miguel, but he outweighed me by at least 40 pounds. I asked if he was a warrior in the spiritual sense or did he actually fight other warriors. With the demeanor of a gentle giant, he volunteered that he had to kill real people who were enemies.

Shaken, I asked who the enemies were. He answered that they were from another tribe. The same tribe that had forced the Maya to leave Palenque 800 years ago.

He seemed very sincere, although, as a warrior, it may have been necessary to conceal the truth.

It was getting surreal when Miguel's son handed me his coup stick. (A coup stick is actually a ceremonial war club, intricately carved and with a diagonal line for each person killed. Native American war leaders from the past often owned a coup stick.) I had never seen a real one. There were three lines on it, indicating he had killed three people. I stammered out a question to the effect of: Did all of the killings cause you to get PTSD? He replied that it had not traumatized him, but rather it had given him more strength and power.

The Maya!

Was I really sitting there with men from a war culture that had never died out? It seemed so. Overall, the conversation was mostly about discovering how much we had in common. Don Fyo and I are both environmentalists at heart and believe that global warming is the biggest threat to humans.

Gloria returned and announced that she was hungry. She had secretly been fending off subtle advances in the car and wanted to leave. Before we drove away, Don Fyo and I embraced and vowed that we were brothers in the Global Revolution! Gloria sat between Luis and me on the way back.

I was very high but somehow remembered all the day's major events as if they were etched into my mind by a diamond. Fyo had also talked about medicinal plants and other shamanic practices, but I forgot most of that inf0rmation. Other than a large tree with red bark, I couldn't remember much of what he told me about medicinal plants. The tree was called *ahe,* and the bark was used for a tea that was good for the heart. He served me some, reassuring me it would help with my irregular heartbeat.

Don Fyo also offers visitors a *temascal,* or sweat bath in the mouth of a cave. There is a mummy somewhere deep inside the underground labyrinth. Scary!

But my attention was focused on his politics and his personality. He is the elder leader of his community, one who has earned the respect of others. He has taught himself to read and has studied Marx. He understands the modern world and is a wise man.

Fyo loved Gloria from the start. The next time we visited, he was having a little party. Gloria danced with him to traditional Mexican music. They looked so cute that I made a video.

That evening, on the return to El Panchan, the young couple rode quietly in the back. They had stayed by themselves during the day. The guy thanked me for paying them a visit while tripping and swimming naked. He said that the weed I'd smoked with him had taken him to the next level. That was all he needed. For him, it was like having a dad who showed up with good advice. Since I have become a guide to all things psychedelic, the young couple felt secure. They will never forget that day!

Most Americans don't understand what a shaman is. The best answer is that they are usually something like a preacher or spiritual leader. But there are many types of shamans in this world. This is because many tribes around the world have kept shamanic traditions alive. It is also because we Westerners are rediscovering our roots. Stonehenge was built at a time when priests were in charge of society!

Being a preacher's kid has taught me that there are as many religious leaders as there are kinds of people. Look at the US. We elected a phony President with his own fake shaman. (If you follow the news, he was the tall guy who wore bull horns on his head and a ridiculous shaman outfit;

the same guy who is now in jail for invading the Capitol on January 6.)

Worlds collide! People die! We are on a planet that is out of balance, and it is our responsibility to fix it.

Back in Panchan, we woke up on our final day. I felt a little melancholy at the thought of leaving. It was cold back in Shasta.

After a quick breakfast at Felicia's, we went hiking to the waterfall. Gloria loved the giant monkey face. We were alone in nature, and the air was full of sounds: the birds, the distant bellowing of monkeys, and the tumbling water.

It was hot by the time we returned to the *cabaña*, so we joined most of the other large primates and lounged around during mid-day. We walked over to Felicia's Restaurant when it cooled off a little. Gloria had already become friends with Felicia. The restaurant is a place where lucky people find freedom from the old rules. Felicia serves great food and somehow has the power to let her restaurant be a place of freedom for her customers. The tables are in the open air, and customers can smoke weed and drink beer.

So we spent the last evening partying with our new friends. Luis and David were there, along with some tourist friends from Europe.

Luis offered me a mushroom, and I thought, "What the hell? It's our last night." So I took it. It was stronger than the ones from before. (One of the guys eventually explained that the last mushroom to grow from the cow shit is the most potent. This occurs when it stops raining for a few days.) I got so high that I stopped feeling social and went off to be alone for a while.

When I returned, Luis was alone with Gloria. They were acting strangely. Luis kept trying to get me to leave.

Meanwhile, every time he tried to send me on an errand, Gloria would tap my foot under the table. Something was up!

When we walked back to the *cabaña*, I asked Gloria what was going on.

She said, "I'll tell you tomorrow."

The next morning, after we drove away from Panchan, she told me that Luis was in love with her. I hadn't seen that coming. He was less than half her age.

She told me that he had been secretly romancing her for days. It appeared that he hadn't taken me seriously when I told him that he really needed to be honest and conduct himself with more integrity. Apparently, he thought I wouldn't find out, but it was a reckless move either way. He did not know if I was dangerous. And Chiapas is a dangerous place.

I try not to be vindictive. It isn't a place to go if you are on "The Path."

The airport was in the capital of Chiapas, called Tuxtla Gutiérrez. It was only about eighty miles from Palenque, but it took all day to drive the circuitous route because the highways are the worst I have ever driven. They are full of potholes, speed bumps, and people.

Many people are walking to the United States from Guatemala and other countries. It's sad because they need help so badly. Who feeds them when they run out of money?

The highway problem is made worse by the Federal Government because the Zapatistas control most of the area. The Feds don't want to repair roads that help their enemies.

So, as a result, you are forced to drive slowly. I found out the hard way.

After arriving in the capital, the plan was to drive through the rebel-controlled parts of Chiapas. I rented a car at the airport. The car was a mess, and one of the tires went flat a few miles from the airport. It took about two hours to repair it, putting us behind schedule.

Once we got on the highway, I was in a hurry. However, the brakes were bad. As we were coming into a town, I was driving too fast to avoid a deep pothole. The brakes locked up, and this slammed the front end into the hole with such force that it broke the radiator.

We were stranded in the town of Comitan, but we soon found a mechanic. He was interesting looking: short and stocky, with long, curly black hair. He was a good mechanic and had been trained in a Zapatista school. I really liked the guy.

When it became obvious that repairs would take days, we gave up and called the rental company. I foresaw some kind of problem like this months before we left California. After a lifetime of experience, I can often "guess" what the future will be like.

I had warned Gloria that we were in for a huge adventure, and there would be a price to pay. It started out like a sixties acid trip, intimidating and disorienting. But we were prepared for the hard part. We had discussed it, and she trusted me. It was the karmic price for a ticket to the wilds of Chiapas.

I had to pay the mechanic for a ride back to San Cristobal De Las Casas. It got dark during the drive. He and his wife quietly spoke an Indigenous language as we sat in the back. They were bilingual.

The towns out in rural Chiapas serve as hubs where various tribes come in from the surrounding countryside to shop and socialize. In these places, the poor are no longer ruled by the rich. Most of the elites were kicked out or killed during the fighting. Some rich people were allowed to keep their property because the rebels respected them.

So we ended up waiting outside a convenience store for hours before the rental company delivered another car. The worst part was that they charged my credit card another $1,800.

That was how the adventure had begun. The return drive was an uneventful success. We had learned a lesson. Don't drive across the state of Chiapas! The rest of the trip home was a blur of airports and other uncomfortable travel.

We had found a new home in the enchanted little enclave of El Panchan, at the gateway to the majesty of Palenque, in the wilds of Chiapas, Mexico.

~~~

So after more visits and more adventures, we have returned to Palenque. It is New Year's Eve, and the rain is pouring down. There is nothing to do but purchase umbrellas and try to stay dry.

As is the jungle. As are the local characters. So we have found a second home here in Panchan. Gloria hangs out with Felicia and her friends when we chill here while I smoke weed with the young people. They are a mixture of local Maya hustlers and young visitors. The visitors have heard of the magic and want to experience it first-hand.

It is into this matrix that Gloria and I return. But with a new goal. We are here to show my children this place. We will find new magic!

Besides Felicia's, there is a large restaurant called Don Mucho's where they have live music. It is the first establishment you see upon arriving in El Panchan. It serves as a buffer between the wild interior and the "straight world."

I once pondered over a group of retired Americans who were dining at Don Mucho's. Large, ugly, and white, they were completely oblivious to their surroundings and had no idea of the possibilities only yards away. They just ate and drank pitchers of margaritas. Imagine how we must look in the eyes of these beautiful, brown people. No wonder we are often known as the "Ugly Americans."

Only little streams and wooden bridges separate the two worlds. The sidewalks on the wild side branch off into strange and exotic places! You may be walking through the jungle and come to a wooden sign that says: "Traditional Toltec Tattoo," with a path leading further on. Felicia's is just over a footbridge from Don Mucho's but hidden in the jungle. If you cross over another small bridge, you discover an outdoor bar owned by a nice German guy named Heinrich. He is married to a Maya woman, and they have kids.

Local hustlers with names like Slim, hang out on the wild side of the bridges and provide services for travelers. People can score anything from mushrooms to hard drugs depending on what's available. The mushrooms grow most months of the year but not during dry spells in the spring. You can even hire some of the guys as a guide or a driver. Jungle Palace keeps the locals out. Otherwise, the partying and dealing would spill over and bother customers.

Further into the jungle, you can rent a cheaper cabaña for about ten dollars. They have no hot water. And no rules on partying there!

The whole thing is kind of like a Mr. Tambourine Man experience. People often play guitars and sing. Others wander around, discovering mysterious places. It's like being in a constant state of euphoria for many young visitors.

Gloria loves Panchan and has developed friendships. Her crowd has fun without the need for drugs. They are the people who run the businesses while the rest of us party. Gloria and I learn from them. They often gossip or provide valuable information.

This is how Gloria learned that Luis was murdered. He had been breaking unwritten rules laid down by *el mafioso*. We found out when we went for a walk by a ranch. There was a pasture full of cows and a big Maya cowboy on a horse. He greeted us from the other side of the fence, so we said, "*Buenas* días." As he was talking to us, we realized that we knew him. It was Juan, a guy who had previously driven us to Don Fyo's. He spoke mostly to Gloria, but I thought he was saying that Luis had been killed. When I asked her about it, tears welled up in her eyes. I didn't know what to say, and Juan just rode away.

It was tragic. It turned out that Luis was married and had a family in San Cristobal De Las Casas.

People in Mexico live with death more than we Americans. Gloria lost two brothers when they were young. Many people believe God or destiny decides your fate. And most people in Mexico don't wear seat belts because they believe wearing them won't matter.

The rain continued pouring down on the jungle. In the morning, the water had nearly reached the foundation of our *cabaña*, but the drops were finally letting up a little. It is amazing how a small stream can swell into a surging torrent in one day!

The family vacation began on New Year's Day 2020. It started out like any normal family vacation. We went to see the great city of Palenque.

My daughter at Monkey Head waterfall

Then we drove to Belize, where cannabis is legal, and people are laid back. It is a little country in the Caribbean, and the people speak English. We got to know some local guys who were great guides. They smoked weed and were more like Jamaicans. It was a totally different experience for us.

But sadly, while we were snorkeling, I could see the coral reefs were dying. The vibrant colors were disappearing. The destruction from global warming is everywhere now.

As that vacation continued, everything began to change: my life, my country, and even the world. It was just before

COVID-19 became a problem and before so many loved ones died.

Don Fyo saw it coming. After returning from Belize, we visited him, and he predicted the changes.

After introductions, we all walked over to a new shrine he had created. It was a small hut filled with artifacts and other shamanic treasures. Then he began to warn us about the future, saying hard times were coming. He said that COVID was going to become a pandemic. (It wasn't even on my radar yet.)

And he warned us about death.

I knew that bad things were coming, but I didn't expect it all to happen so fast. Fyo had somehow "seen" the future, and it had arrived! But we knew that we were safe with him, and we were living in the moment.

How brief the moment would be!

After spending some time at the river, Gloria visited with Don Fyo and Juan, who was our driver again. After the mushrooms had worn off a little bit, I joined them.

The four of us had also been with Juan on the previous day. He had driven us to the house of a guy who held ayahuasca ceremonies. He wasn't home, but his wife came out and told us that he was in Germany.

We were driving through the backside of the same big pasture where Juan had been riding the horse a few days earlier. I asked him where the mushrooms grew, and without hesitation, he pointed to a lush, low spot next to us and said, "Right there."

Cool. I had been wondering if they were growing right under everyone's noses. The main road passes right on one side of this field, so the answer was yes.

A couple of minutes later, he turned off the main road to show us his house. As we got out of the car, his teenage son pushed a wheelbarrow out of the field. It contained over a hundred psilocybin mushrooms placed on a large sheet of paper. Amazing! This was just the kind of tourism I wanted my kids to experience. The regular tourists were just looking at the giant pyramids while we were nearby in mushroom land acquiring some to eat at Don Fyo's place. Underground tourism.

My daughters with the wheelbarrow full of fresh mushrooms

So it became the natural choice to have Juan be our driver to visit Don Fyo. Although we had eaten less than half of our mushrooms, my offspring were still high when they returned from the river. They said hello to us but then began chasing fireflies. The cute little bugs were a novelty to them.

We were all hungry when we got back to Panchan, so we went to eat at Felicia's. My daughter Michelle loved the traditional Maya tortillas made out of *maiz* and filled with sweet potatoes and other vegetables. After eating, Michelle and her younger sibling, Jamie, planned to have drinks at Heinrich's bar. It was open, with its usual mix of young visitors drinking and smoking. Customers loved the freedom and openness of the atmosphere there.

When I walked by on my way back to the *cabaña*, Heinrich told me my kids had just ordered drinks. I looked all around, but they were not visible. He insisted they were there, but they were on the ground behind a group at a table. And there they were. With a sick and starving puppy! They looked desperate as they huddled over that puppy. That was the moment when life changed.

"Dad, we have to help him!"

"But Sweetie, there are puppies like that all over Mexico."

They didn't want to hear it. Their fear turned briefly to anger. They were laser-focused on the puppy. Both are animal lovers, and they had never seen a puppy in such bad shape. He could barely walk. Near starvation and suffering from multiple diseases, he looked pitiful. But he was still cute, as all puppies are. He was a mutt, a patchwork, with short hair of varying shades from beige and muted yellow to black. His goofy ears were floppy, and he had a sweet face. He was a few months old and should have been of a bigger size, but he only weighed about ten pounds.

He was a survivor with DNA passed down from countless generations of survivors. Though almost a jungle dog, he was not one of the Maya's hairless ones. They are a breed called Xoloitzcuintli. (Don't ask me how to pronounce that name.) Being hairless, they are less likely to get skin diseases. To Americans, the dogs appear creepy at first because they have bald skin instead of fur. The weird part is getting used to petting their skin. They feel human. You don't know whether to pet them or massage them. Generally very sweet, they seem to have the demeanor of a big hound. But this little guy in front of us did have hair. It was all falling out because he had several skin diseases.

The situation was almost hopeless. I felt as sorry for my kids as for the puppy. Doing damage control for sounding uncaring, I suggested we buy him some chicken from Felicia's.

After feeding him, we carried him over to the creek and put him in shallow water so he could drink. Instead, he fell over. He was very weak.

The entire end of our vacation would focus on him. And saving the little guy would help soothe the pain of tragedy.

My children took him back to their *cabaña* for the night and made him a little bed. Michelle put all her powers to work in the morning and arranged to save the puppy. She found a veterinarian and made plans to have him adopted by friends. We all took him to the vet before my kids left for Mexico City. Gloria and I would be flying home a few days later.

As usual, I was up early, saying, "Hi" to Gladys as I passed the office at Jungle Palace. It was a cool morning, and the sun was rising somewhere above the jungle foliage, but it wasn't reaching the ground yet. As I was passing the open kiosk, my phone rang. It was Michelle calling from Mexico City. I immediately knew by her tone that something terrible had happened.

"Dad."

"What happened, Sweetie?"

"Mike was killed last night."

"No! No! No! Oh no!"

She was crying.

It was such a shock that I couldn't talk and had to call her back later. I was spinning in circles, with Gladys watching and wondering. I told her my stepson had been killed. Then I walked back to the *cabaña* and told Gloria. We were in shock for a while.

My first thought was that he might have relapsed and overdosed after years of sobriety. But later, Michelle explained that he had been run over while riding a motorcycle. The guy who killed him was high on drugs.

Michelle was devastated; they had a special bond that only close siblings can have. He was her half-brother, and they were as close as adult siblings can be. She had him visit her often and paid for everything they did together. Even though he was ten years older, she had become a second mom to him. They really loved each other.

Being in Mexico helped us a little with the pain of losing Michael. We were in a different part of the world. Also, Michelle and I began talking about how Don Fyo had told us to prepare for tragedy. We had been warned that things were about to go wrong. And through some mystical twist of fate, we now had a puppy to save. We could symbolically save one life to replace another.

Run away! But not forever, as your peers have, hiding

in their white homes. Only run long enough to escape from the pain that accompanies the loss of a loved one. Michael would have wanted me to keep on being happy, continue celebrating life, and partying. I didn't deserve the respect he gave me.

Mike didn't really party much anymore. A little, at the end of his life, when he was trying to escape again. He was starting to hear voices haunting him because of his past. He told me about the voices, and I told him to try to ignore them. He blamed it on the evils of prison, the drugs, and the regrets. In the past couple of years, he had stopped communicating with me. Maybe it was because he didn't want me to see him slipping into the darkness.

But he was beautiful, and everybody loved him. His memorial was a huge, elaborate service. He was sincere and kind, he did not judge others, and was a natural leader. He had the looks of Brad Pitt and a soft kind of power, backed by a charismatic personality. He "walked softly and carried a big stick."

His pain is over. We all failed him.

Why are some of us lucky? After all this trauma, where is my PTSD? A psychologist once told me that choosing to live in nature is an escape caused by Post Traumatic Stress Disorder. Okay. Great!

And maybe psychedelic drugs really do help a person escape from it. There is scientific evidence that cannabis does. Great!

Run away, little boy! Run to your Mother. She is always ready to comfort you. Pacha Mama!

I named the puppy Pachito in honor of El Panchan. A month later, I returned to Palenque to bring him to California. He was healthier, so I bought a leash and took him for walks around the Panchan community. Because of his story and his name, he became quite a local celebrity. We would walk by Felicia's or Don Mucho's, and people would call out his name and tell his story to others.

Pachito was crafty and sophisticated for his age. He was "street smart." His long ears flopped when he walked somewhat resembling a little brown pig. But in spite of his ears, he walked with newfound pride and confidence. It was the first time in his life that he could be a normal puppy. He wasn't wandering around trying to find food. Everyone in Panchan loved him.

He had a sibling people had told me about. I once saw it wandering around near the park entrance. It was standing in the road and looked just like Pachito. A few days later, it was killed by a car.

Because the COVID-19 epidemic had begun, I could not bring Pachito back to California. But a sympathetic veterinarian eventually found him a home with a teacher and his family. I hope he is ok.

9

MESSENGERS

It is time to escape from here. "Mother Nature, please cure my wounds. Paradise is waiting on the other side of this troubled morning. Make a run for it!"

I have been awakened by a nightmare that I was trapped in a city and with no clear avenue of escape for many years. The nightmare had arrived. But like long ago, I am not sleeping today. It's real!

My childhood wasn't always easy, either. In those days, society generally ignored family violence. My older brother and my dad were violent with me. But I always escaped it into the woods. Nature has been my sanctuary ever since.

I made a mistake that quickly drained away my medicine and caused terrible stress. It was my nightmare with a woman named Lisa, that I will soon describe. I had to escape, and I could only pray that sleep deprivation wouldn't cause me to lose it. "Runaway, fool!"

My friends were arriving in Ensenada. After six months of trying to convince somebody to come to Baja, my buddy John was flying to San Diego. We were planning to attend Tata Kachora's Solstice Dance.

His friend Paul has a house south of Ensenada, and they invited me down for a visit. The house is in Uruapan's quaint town on "The Old Wine Route."

I accepted their offer and drove down from Ensenada. The city seemed to sprawl south endlessly. The highway was terrible due to smoke-belching trucks, potholes, and stoplights. There appeared to be an endless row of Walmarts and Costco stores. We couldn't enter a rural area until the last few miles.

Once you escape the congestion and enter the countryside, a feeling of relief begins to set in. The village of Uruapan looks like a picture of Tuscany, complete with those tall, narrow cypress trees. It's pastoral and lovely. Wineries grace the low, rolling hills. There is a hot springs resort in the middle of the valley. The house we stayed in had no hot water, so we bathed at the resort. It had the kind of water that didn't smell like rotten eggs and was good for bathing. A bath costs thirty pesos, or about a dollar fifty. The place was peaceful.

The bath was the last relaxing moment for a couple of days. I had been setting myself up for a crisis but didn't see it coming.

Part of the problem concerned Tata Kachora.

Sadly, I have not gone to see him for over two months. Things were getting messy. The people around him told me to pay a lot of cash and have a legal contract before I could continue writing. We had a handshake deal when he had originally asked me to write about him. Nobody placed limits on what I was to talk about. I knew only that Tata Kachora wanted the book to be about his history and knowledge of plants. So I immediately started writing, working with what I knew. Going back and changing it would be complicated and make it a different book.

I had just spent thousands of dollars on his house's solar system, and nobody thanked me. I don't blame Tata Kachora. This was more of an issue with his family members and younger students. It would take having free electricity before they would appreciate the benefits of having a solar system, both practically and symbolically. The truth is that they are like most people and have not incorporated the paradigm shift (sustainability, etc.) into daily life.

However, Thiago and the others had given me permission to write until the solar project was completed. So I have chosen to stop there. This will be a short book.

The whole thing became like a game of chess. The king didn't move much, so his knights and bishops controlled most of the action. Tata Kachora is not in control of the details of his life. He is probably too old. Younger people usually take over the details concerning business decisions.

I asked a lot of people for advice on whether or not to pay the money, and they all said no. Some people who offered advice were insiders. They offered me different perspectives. Asking them questions filled in more of Tata Kachora's story, even giving me a clearer picture of his relationship with Castaneda. They are people who have been close to him in the years since Castaneda.

Yet, at this point, it's starting to feel like the fog of war is closing in. I must tell you that if you look deep into the question: "Who was Don Juan?" no one could claim that title.

Tata Kachora himself even told me that Don Juan does not exist. Scholars also agree that there was not just one person who taught Castaneda all the information he attributes to Don Juan. As a nonexclusive (and not particularly scientific) anthropologist, he had been learning and intermingling ideas from many teachers. But it makes sense that Castaneda would have selected a real person to focus on. And it needed to be someone who was accessible and had a unique and interesting personality. Believe me, Tata Kachora's personality is unique in all the world. He is truly one of a kind!

My friend, Tata Oso, told me he was there when Tata Kachora accepted the idea that he had been Castaneda's model. A German man named Bert Hellinger attended Oso's Dance, along with Tata Kachora. Oso heard Hellinger tell Tata Kachora that he was Castaneda's, Don Juan. At first, Tata Kachora replied that he wasn't Don Juan. But later, he admitted to being the person Castaneda had described. As usual, the color of truth is not black and white. It's gray! He had decided to come out of the closet when he admitted to Hellinger that he was Castaneda's man.

I honestly believe that Tata Kachora was Castaneda's primary source and inspiration. After all, he has told me that many of Castaneda's narratives were true, but not all. I have even asked him obscure questions that only he could answer. One question required knowledge of geography and history that only he and I would likely possess.

A passage in one of the books always had special meaning to me. Castaneda and Don Juan were driving past a place called "Los Vidrios," and Castaneda recorded the conversation. (A separate reality" by Carlos Castaneda, Chapter 3 page 33)

Soon after I read about it, I found myself at Los Vidrios. In the 1970s, it was the only place you could eat and gas up between San Luis and Sonoita. It was an outpost in the middle of the unforgiving Sonoran Desert: an oasis with beer, Coke, and food. In those days, it was also the gateway to Pinacate.

Los Vidrios is gone now. It is just a ruin. I watched it crumble to the ground during the 1990s.

Returning to the conversation between Castaneda and Don Juan while driving past Los Vidrios, Castaneda asked Don Juan why they called the place Los Vidrios or The Glass? He then suggested that it was probably because of all the volcanic glass in the area. However, Don Juan replies that it is named The Glass because a glass truck once crashed there. He explained that Mexicans would not name it after the volcano glass because they did not have any interest in a distant-looking, dark mountain and wouldn't have known about it.

So I asked him about the passage and if it was accurate. He told me that the two had passed Los Vidrios, and it was true. Then he said, "Pinacate is very beautiful." This is a strong indication that he had been to Pinacate. (Some of the other shamans and students have never been to Pinacate and are waiting for me to take them next winter.)

I am sure that Tata Kachora knows more about Sonora than I do. We have discussed his gradual migration from the Yaqui territory to Baja. As a teenager, he moved with his grandparents to Hermosillo, where they opened a store selling native plants. *"Una botánica."* He worked as a lumberjack, cutting mesquite trees.

This makes sense because his grandparents would have found a way to return home after being exiled to Southern Mexico.

He told me that his next move was to Caborca, where he briefly opened a *botanica*. Caborca is very close to Pinacate. He knew how to gather his own plants because his parents had taught him. He probably visited Pinacate during this period to collect plants.

I am saying here that, as part scientist and part insider, I am seeing into this. First, it is a fact that Tata Kachora knew Carlos Castaneda. He identified Castaneda in a photograph and two Huichol shamans named Ramon Medina and Jose Rios.

An anthropologist named Jay C. Fikes had shown Tata Kachora the photo. Fikes was trying to track down the real Don Juan. But he focused on the Huichol shamans and the peyote ceremonies. He also earned his doctoral degree in the process.

Fikes wrote a book called *Carlos Castaneda, Academic Opportunism and the Psychedelic Sixties*. In it, Fikes doesn't investigate Tata Kachora much as a source for Don Juan. He believed the character was based on several teachers who Castaneda knew but primarily focused on Ramon Medina.

I think Fikes got it wrong and threw the baby out with the bathwater. Tata Kachora was the main person behind the "Don Juan character." Here is my argument:

We know that Tata Kachora knew Fikes and Medina. This shows that Tata Kachora could have been Castaneda's Don Juan because he was there.

The picture and the fact that Fikes tells us that Tata Kachora identified the men show that Castaneda was learning something from all of them. In this sense, their knowledge went into the mosaic that Fikes and others believed was Castaneda's mythical Don Juan.

However, Fikes stated that the peyote ceremony Castaneda attended was not a part of Tata Kachora's knowledge because it was, in fact, a Huichol ceremony. He concluded that Tata Kachora was not involved.

Now, this is where an insider perspective is useful. Tata Kachora and his peers learned ceremonies from other shamans and other tribes and later provided them to the public.

"Tata Kachora and family invite you to the medicine ceremony through our ancient traditions of the red path."

I intuitively realized it at Tata Kachora's Spring Dance when it appeared to be based on the Lakota Sioux Dances. Later, Tata Oso confirmed it when he said that he was the one who taught Tata Kachora how to put on a Spring Dance. Oso had learned it from the Lakota Sioux in South Dakota many years ago.

From what we now know, it makes sense to assume that Medina or another Huichol turned Tata Kachora on to peyote. Castaneda would have participated in a Huichol Peyote Ceremony because Fikes proved the ceremony described by Castaneda was a Huichol ceremony. But that doesn't mean Tata Kachora didn't lead his own peyote ceremonies or co-lead them with a Huichol. We know that Tata Kachora learns ceremonies from other tribes and makes them his own. He still holds peyote ceremonies. This proves that a big part of Fikes's thesis is wrong. (See Tata Kachora's invitation to a recent peyote ceremony.) Why did Fikes assume that because Tata Kachora was a Yaqui, he could not hold a peyote ceremony? Didn't Fikes even spend time with Tata Kachora in Sonora?

We can see that when we really start to dig in and look, there is only one good candidate for the Don Juan character. Tata Kachora was based in the Tijuana area at the time, easily accessible to Castaneda. Opposingly, the Huichol villages were extremely difficult to reach at the time. So Castaneda would not have been able to make the journey very often. There is also a great deal of documentation showing that Castaneda visited Tata Kachora twelve to sixteen times.

Another good piece of the puzzle that fits is regarding the Datura plant. Castaneda spent a lot of time describing how Don Juan had taught him about it. Datura is very common in Sonora and Baja, and Tata Kachora still teaches students about it. A current student who is a friend of mine was taught the same information as Castaneda. So both the Datura plant and Lophophora, the peyote cactus, continue to be part of Tata Kachora's teachings. It all adds up. Things that appear really mysterious and convoluted can be understood with the help of education, intuition, and an inside scoop.

Tata Kachora is the main personality described in the books. His personality is the same. The Red Path is the same. The plants are the same.

Now let's consider this: At some point, Tata Kachora himself could have read a Castaneda book, possibly because Castaneda wrote that he had given Don Juan a copy.

So when Tata Kachora read the book, he realized that it was pieced together and included Castaneda's experiences with other people and situations. Thus, Tata Kachora would have been reluctant to claim he was Don Juan.

On the other hand, Tata Kachora would have an impossible task if he were an impostor. How could anyone assume a fake identity when they are in their 90s? Also, he would not talk about the Red Path with such compassion. He would not speak with real anger and betrayal in his voice every time Castaneda came up. He would be the greatest imposter of all time, and I would be a fool.

I am betting he is not an imposter. Did I figure it out? People can decide for themselves. The evidence I offer here should be proof enough for most readers. There will be many skeptics. But it would require an exhaustive review of all the evidence to satisfy the social scientists and the skeptic in us all. The fact that there is so much mystery involved in Tata Kachora's story only makes it richer and more magical. Look at his website.

The Red Path is my path once again. I feel like I have largely defeated the enemies of fear, power, and clarity. So there is only one enemy left for me. The last enemy, old age, is my last battle.

This is how I keep myself busy as the world collapses around me! Thank you, Tata Kachora, for giving me a purpose again. Better than turning into a fucking Trump zombie, like some of my friends.

Death as an advisor! This is Toltec thinking from long ago. Any good Don Juan from the group would have thought about it, but Castaneda was the one who shared it with us.

"My only friend, the end." Jim Morrison, 1966. "Come on, Baby, run with me!"

~~~

When I returned to Ensenada for a dental implant in early June and drove by Grandfather's house again, because of his young advisers, I didn't feel welcome without paying for a contract. It was stressful because I also wanted to attend the Solstice Dance with my friends but did not. Things would soon get worse.

The hills were drying out, and the heat was intense. The whole West has been in the grip of the worst heatwave ever! Global warming has devastated Baja even more than the rest of California. But some spots had gotten rain in May. Those places were green, and lots of flowers were blooming.

Down I went, through the timeless little villages and, later, the Wine Route. After cresting a final pass, the Pacific Ocean appeared in the distance. The temperature started to drop quickly. It was a welcome escape from the heat.

As usual, Ensenada was partly cloudy and lovely. Poncho happened to be home, so I stopped in for a nice visit. My dental appointment was in the morning.

I had big plans for later. Marco invited me to camp at the Ceremonial Site controlled by Tata Oso, or "Grandfather Bear." It is in the high country, near La Rumorosa, just a few miles south of the US border. I headed there after my appointment. The drive takes three hours and passes Tata Kachora's house.

Marco told me that a friend of his was eager to meet me. Lisa was part of the informal community at the Site and knew everyone who frequented the ceremonies. Marco thought Lisa and I had a lot in common because she learned about plant medicine.

The high temperature has averaged a dry 95° F at the Site this summer. So it was hot when I got to the area and tried to find the Site. I had only been there once or twice and hadn't memorized the route.

After driving around for 30 minutes, I backtracked and located Tata Oso's place.

His stepson, Angel, was there, and Oso had left him an old Ford truck to drive, so I followed him down the dirt roads and to the Site. Not surprisingly, I was the first one to arrive, and I was two hours late. Arrival times are very casual in Mexico.

I parked next to the only building, which serves as a kitchen and social hall. Then I walked around looking for the best place to camp. There was a perfect spot next to a long boulder surrounded by pines and juniper trees. The trees received extra water from the rain running off the side of the boulder. The best thing about the camp was that it provided privacy because it was off by itself.

The area has some of the most beautiful scenery in the West. It consists of flat areas broken by low ridges of granite. The boulders are often sitting on larger boulders. Then you have the most exotic mixture of cactuses and trees growing in between. Many similar places exist, including some around Lake Tahoe and Mount Whitney, but none prettier than this. It is a sacred place.

It was hot as I set up camp, but with plenty of shade and a breeze. I was alone with my thoughts. There was time to figure out what to do. I had just met with one of *their* lawyers in Ensenada, and he assured me that he could write up a contract that would be agreeable to everyone involved. But during the discussion, he told me something that stuck in my mind. One of Tata Kachora's students had drawn up a contract to write a book. But it was right after I had started mine, and he knew it.

The lawyer didn't realize what this information meant to me. This was not The Red Path to me. It smelled more like a sneaky business deal.

The Earth and my intuition would guide me as they always do. They are the same thing anyway. But it threw me into doubt again, and I decided not to give them any money until I could figure it out. Besides, I was headed to a place where I could find out more information.

But I was alone until people started showing up. However, some of them would eventually volunteer advice and information.

People were arriving and setting up distant camps. Eventually, I saw a woman walking toward my camp and figured it must be Lisa. She had blond hair and a light complexion, like the woman in the picture Marco had texted me.

She introduced herself, and I offered her my only chair. She declined the chair but accepted my offer to smoke a joint. However, clear communication was difficult because it was hard to understand her Spanish, and she rarely spoke English. I felt a little awkward around her from the start but hoped it would get better with time. She may have felt the same way.

Finally, Marco showed up with his wife and two boys. Felicia, his wife, is beautiful and charming. The ten-year-old is called Junior, and he was chosen as the best ten-year-old soccer player in Arizona. Marco and his dad, Tavo, along with Junior, are a local soccer dynasty. Even the three-year-old already plays on a team. Marco and Tavo both coach the kids' teams. Poor Felicia has to listen to talk about *fútbol* all the time.

Other people began arriving. Some were regulars at the Site, and others were new. In all, there were about twenty people. Tata Oso was holding a *temescal* in the morning, and a group of women from Mexicali had arrived for their first one.

A *temescal* is like a worship service, but much more because it involves a sweat lodge. It is truly a cleansing and curative ceremony. The shamans I have met focus on the sacredness of Earth when they preach. God is more nebulous because the participants usually come from a past involving traditional churches. The leaders don't want to offend people by challenging their beliefs.

In the morning, I chose to go hiking instead of attending the *temescal*. I didn't want to stress my heart in the steam. But I participated in the ceremony where everyone held hands in a circle before entering the lodge. The energy around it was pure and cleansing.

The landscape was one in which the high plateau was occasionally broken up by ridges and mountains as it rose. The Site was located near the beginning of a ridge. The granite boulders were the most striking feature of the landscape. All shapes and sizes of them spilled out onto the flat areas and adorned the rising ridges. The most exotic plants and animals lived in the boulders. The place looked magical!

It was hot when I returned from exploring the area. The women were bathing the old-fashioned way by hauling buckets of water from the well. There were little shelters made for bathing and a few outhouses around. The place had turned into a little community.

After the *temescal* ended, Oso drove Marco and me around and showed us the lots that he was selling. The lots started on the ridge, and two bordered the Site itself. Many of the lots were spectacular. Many had boulders up to twenty feet high. A few days later, I bought the two lots bordering the Site. Marco and Felicia bought a lot in a flat area with giant boulders.

Now I can sit on a boulder and look down at ceremonies. My land covers over an acre but seems even larger. Most of it is covered with boulders and trees, but there is a flat area by the dirt road.

In the afternoon, about twelve people all piled into Marco's big truck and headed to a nearby lake. The water was great for swimming, but if you left your legs in the water too long, the sunfish would nibble on them. I'm kind of used to it. Now it is all the rage at expensive spas. Everyone had a good time swimming and exploring.

One of the major personalities at the Site was a guy named Mapuche. He was in his sixties, had long hair,

My new land above the Ceremonial Site.

and looked cool. He had arrived with a younger woman friend who had several kids. He was a student of the Toltec tradition and sometimes led *temescals*.

Mapuche was a refugee from Chile who had been in a revolution during the 1970s. During that time, the President, named Pinochet, was murdering leftists. People told me that Mapuche preferred being with his three German shepherds to being with people. He had worked in the US and spoke English. Like me, he smokes weed, wears his hair long, and has a strong personality. We get along out of mutual respect.

We are now elders and have Medicine.

Around the time I wondered how people with such powerful personalities could coexist, something happened.

I heard someone shout outside the kitchen.

Tempers do boil over.

Later, Lisa told me that she and Mapuche had gotten into an argument. Boom! Red flag! They didn't always coexist peacefully here.

Later in the afternoon, as we sat around my camp trying to communicate, I was already wondering if there was a possibility of developing a connection between Lisa and me. I didn't feel any chemistry. Did she? But she was crazy excited to visit Mount Shasta and wanted to get to know me.

She claimed to be free from responsibilities. So I agreed to meet her in Ensenada in a few days. We planned to visit the highest mountains in Baja – a national park called San Pedro De Mártir. Then we would go to Tata Kachora's Solstice Dance.

The truth is that Marco had thought we might get together and had spent time telling both of us that we had a lot in common. We did, so both of us were interested.

At this time, I was seriously considering buying the land. It would mean that I could also be a part of the community. (And as I mentioned above, I did end up buying two lots.) The weekend was a lot of fun, and I could relate to the people at the camp. We were there for a common purpose. And it connected us to the Earth.

However, as the world has veered into chaos, it has become harder and harder for me to engage in small talk with people. Most people haven't adapted and aren't doing anything to stop climate change. But change *is* happening now. I live in the "now."

That leaves me with few friends: Poncho, Marco, and my last two American buddies. It's really scary that I cannot be around my family members or other middle-class whites without getting very concerned. They are living in a dream. But it is not "The Dream of The Earth" that Father Thomas Berry described in his book of the same name. No! It is the dream of our crumbling twentieth-century paradigm. Why can't they let go of this dream that has become a nightmare? Probably for the same reason that a frog will not crawl out of water that is growing too hot.

Folks, the reality is that our money can't help us if we don't use it to stop climate change. We are all in this together. I don't have much money, but I have managed to provide three solar systems for myself and others. People often advise me to stop spending money on solar and save it for the future. What kind of future would that be?

We will now return to my existential crisis in Ensenada and the beginning of this chapter:

On Sunday afternoon, everyone was packing up to return to hellish cities, such as Mexicali, that were sweltering in the heat. Lisa and I arranged to meet in Ensenada a few days later. So in the meantime, I drove down to meet my old American buddy John and his friend Paul in Uruapan. Remember, after that last relaxing hot springs bath, I began to lose my balance. Here is how.

First, I offered to drive John to a dental appointment in Ensenada. The round trip drive stressed me out because I couldn't avoid all the potholes, and the traffic was terrible. They need more freeways in Mexico.

Then, Lisa kept changing plans, which kept me a little off balance. We had been planning to attend Tata Kachora's Solstice Dance. I had to brave the highway again because she decided not to meet me near Uruapan. I was already stressed by the time I got to Ensenada.

We met at the parking lot of Playa Bonita, a beach at the north end of town. Everyone was ready to walk on the beach after driving so much, so we climbed down to the tide. It is a special kind of beach because it is steep and covered with round rocks. Every time a big wave comes, it washes thousands of rocks up onto the beach, and they make a loud, clattering noise as they roll back. We enjoyed the beach, but it was the only fun I had with her.

Lisa had arrived with her twelve-year-old daughter and two dogs. Then she informed me that she needed to go to Tijuana for work instead of following through with the plan to visit the national park. Was this her idea of being free of responsibilities?

We had dinner, and then I rented them a room in my hotel. During our awkward conversations, she showed little interest in me. There were no questions about my ideas. The topic she enjoyed most was telling me about how she provided mushrooms, peyote, and organic DMT to clients in healing sessions. This would be fine if she had more experience, but she was a loose cannon, with only five years of experience with "Power Plants."

I had realized my mistake by the time I had rented the room for her. The hotel did not allow pets, but they let me rent the room because I was a good client and had become acquainted with the lady who managed it.

The dogs were shedding all over the bedspreads. They barked a lot, and every time I heard them, it made me cringe. She fed them by pouring the food directly on the lobby floor.

I barely slept all night.

After a late breakfast, we decided to go to the beach. While her daughter was playing in the surf, Lisa appeared happy and affectionate, even touching me. But if I touched her, she would say, "Don't touch me!"

Mixed signals and red flags were popping up all over. We almost argued when I asked why she touched me, then snapped at me if I touched her.

Sitting on that beach towel with her suddenly felt very wrong. Communication broke down even more. I couldn't read her and know what she was really thinking.

She got up and started a sand drawing featuring a heart and flowers. I decided to walk to an outhouse. My stress was so bad that I knew trouble had arrived. I wanted out!

Then something happened that confirmed my feelings. A dog snuck up behind me and bit my bare leg.

At first, I was angry and yelled, "where are the police?" Then I yelled at the dumbass guys drinking beer, standing by their truck. They didn't punish the dog but said they were sorry. I said that's not good enough. "If this was the United States, your dog would be put down, and you would be in trouble."

The blood ran down my leg as I entered the outhouse. I could hear the fools leaving. They would be back after the Gringo went home.

Walking down the beach, the dog bite actually began to feel better. It didn't hurt that much, and I saw it as a confirmation. Lisa was big trouble, and the dog was a messenger. I was bleeding on the outside, but the real pain was on the inside.

It was time to go home. Pacha Mama, you are calling. Cure my wounds.

By the second morning of my ordeal, I was completely exhausted and didn't feel I owed Lisa anything because she had talked about herself the whole time. So I waited until she appeared in the lobby and said goodbye. I drove to Tata Oso's Site in the high country with the last of my strength.

His home was only two miles from the Site, so I went by to see if he could show me the lots again. He did. The lots begin on a small ridge and sprawl across a small horseshoe-shaped valley to the west. Most lots slope up the ridge, but some are on the valley floor. I bought the first two. The land starts at the top of the Site and goes down the backside until it flattens out. It is even prettier than the ranch I just sold to my cousin in Mount Shasta. One could sit on top of one of these boulders and watch a ceremony taking place below.

I camped for three days, healing. A kit fox trotted right past me on the second morning, showing off a giant woodrat in its mouth.

Later, Marco came by for a visit and gave me some medicine. But mostly, I was alone, marveling at the scenery. The only place in California of similar beauty is Joshua Tree National Park. My place is even prettier because more exotic plants are nestled among the boulders.

10
SANCTUARIES

I was at one of my sanctuaries called Medicine Lake Volcano, right behind the more famous Mt. Shasta. The wildfire smoke wasn't too bad there. My camp was at a pond called Blanche Lake. It was about halfway dried up, but still nice. The water was clear except for all the tadpoles, water dogs, and other harmless creatures swimming around.

After having coffee in the morning, I went for a walk to Bullseye Lake. It's a quick five minute walk. My only companion was a bald eagle. At least that would be the human perspective. I know that I'm actually just another animal surrounded by an almost infinite number of other organisms. They all have a purpose. Mine is this writing.

Gloria came back a little into my life at this point – hoping to keep a connection between Leo and me. She brought Leo up here. It was his first camping trip. It is a good sign that he didn't seem to think there was anything too special about being the only people at a lake and being able to swim anytime. He lived on the Klamath River and there are no other houses nearby. The water temperature was about 78°F. Warm. So we played in it and chased the tadpoles and water dogs.

They left yesterday after camping one night. As usual, I was alone. The only sound was from the birds. And sometimes there was no sound. The birds got really noisy around dawn and dusk. Last night, I sat in a flutter of wings as the birds all came down to the little lake for a drink. A bright yellow tanager flew right past me. I was literally surrounded by fluttering. Then it was over and everything became quiet.

This morning it was the woodpeckers that were the loudest. The big Pileated Woodpeckers were here and sounded like somebody hitting a tree with a ball peen hammer. The small ones sounded like the common ones we hear more often. I could see them in my mind, but not with my eyes.

The bald eagle was perched on the tree, waiting to spot a fish. It normally hunted when the first sunlight hit the lake. But there were no fish to be seen. It was hot and they were all hiding on the bottom. They were trying to keep their bodies cool enough to survive. I hoped this heat wave didn't cause my old eagle friend to starve. Bullseye Lake was my Walden Pond. Most of the time there were no people here. It was an emerald gem.

As this year has developed, things have been getting more chaotic. It has been a sacrifice. No Gloria. No Tata Kachora. No home. Just smoke in the woods. With a lot more on the way! How could I escape this?

Was writing a book my last and greatest diversion? Or would I be granted another chapter. I feel the Grim Reaper closing in again!

I was now back in Ensenada already and it had only been a week since Medicine Lake. I was getting my last tooth implant. After this, I was headed up to the mountains because it was going to rain and I wanted to reach my property in time. I felt it.

While driving towards the mountains, two giant cumulonimbus clouds had appeared on the horizon. In the Southwest, the monsoon rains generally begin during July. At least they used to before it became so dry.

Maybe this year the monsoon season would return to the deserts. I was excited after not seeing more than a splash of rain for months. The usual pattern was that clouds began developing at about ten in the morning and continued growing until a thunderstorm broke out somewhere. The storm clouds grew until late afternoon, when they would slowly dissipate. The moisture that was left over often collected into one big thunderstorm at night. It was late morning and the clouds were big and tall. Rain was likely!

It took a lot of concentration when you were trying to haul-ass in Mexico. The driving speeds were normally much slower in Mexico. The rules were different and there were obstacles on the road. But it is fun if you dial it up a notch and change your speedometer to kilometers per hour. It makes you focus even better when you're more aware of the fact that you're going above the speed limit in a country where it's dangerous to drive. I don't do it very often, and I wouldn't recommend driving fast in Mexico to anyone. You also have to be much more aware because there's so many things happening on the roads and highways. In the US, it's much more orderly.

If you are sleepy, it's really scary. It's like one of those times you know you shouldn't be falling asleep because you're in danger, but you can't help it. Yeah, that's exactly what it's like down here when you're tired and you're driving.

Right on cue, I passed a cop giving a guy a ticket for speeding, when I was going 110 in an 80 km/h speed limit area. But it is exciting if you have enough experience and stay focused. Lose your focus, lose your life!

If you paid attention to the news, it seemed that climate change was finally the big topic. Finally! It took unprecedented fires and drought for years before the critical mass was reached. I never dreamed I would be living in a time when climate change took over. Originally, scientists thought it would take longer to get this bad! It is strange to live in the disaster they predicted long ago. It wasn't supposed to happen yet.

Now I can only run and dodge the smoke and the heat. What about the poor people in Mexicali and Phoenix? Also, the elderly? The many who died all over the West because they couldn't afford air conditioning?

I arrived at my property just as the rain was letting up. It rained almost an inch according to the official records. This area was one of the few places not experiencing much drought in the entire West. From here to Tucson, it's wet. There is not much of a drought along the border, but it is the only place in the Southwest that may survive intact during this horror for another year.

After the rain, everything smells so fresh. I may have to follow the rains to keep from getting depressed. The monsoons have returned this year and Arizona is so wet that the fires have gone out. But in California, the western half is bone dry.

Camping was sweet. I had friends. Marco's family and some other Mexican friends were there. His wife Felicia and their kids are super. Lisa was even there and we managed to get past the past. The women were thrilled to be there during the monsoon. They had been cooped up with the kids down in the desert where high temperatures had been averaging 115°F. The weather was soft and damp, without getting too wet. This place was a sanctuary.

Tata Oso held a temescal on Sunday morning. Church.

~~~

I am on the way home now. This highway, 395, passes through what may be the most beautiful countryside in the U.S. I am headed up the backside of the Sierra Nevada Mountains. I used to live nearby in Bishop, but it was a long time ago. I am camping on the Owens River. The view of the Buttermilk Country is spectacular, but something is missing. No snow is left, not even glaciers. Tears well up in my eyes. But I am still alive and the rocks will last. Something new will begin.

My cousin has bought my ranch and I have started moving out. It's going to be hot today. The weather report said there's a slight chance of thunderstorms so I drove up Mount Eddy, where I thought it would rain. The road was good and it didn't take long to drive up there. It was beautiful and it would also provide a nice place to work.

I arrived and it was noon. The sky was a little smoky from forest fires in the distance, but otherwise it had been a fairly clear morning. We were lucky to have so little smoke here today. Most of the West was drenched in smoke again.

A small cloud was beginning to build up right above me. I was going to take a break from writing and watch the clouds grow. It was a beautiful thing to witness. In the mountains, you're not as far below the clouds, so everything happens faster. I'll report back.

The first thunder clap happened almost exactly at two.

A few drops of rain fell. It was a good day to be up here writing. I love this Earth! She gives me what I asked for. Now another clap on the other side of me, two minutes later. All hell was about to break loose on this ridge.

It had been less than an hour total since that cloud began to develop, but I was already starting to think about how long it would take me to walk back to my car because it could really start raining hard soon.

Dry lightning caused a fire right near me and now I was watching planes drop pink fire retardant to put it out before it could get much bigger. Fires were everywhere!

The woods had been my home for many years. The fires had destroyed so much that I felt almost homeless. Nothing lasts forever, but it's hard to watch.

For six months, much of my energy had been consumed by this project. I didn't pay Tata Kachora and the "Young Guns." It would have gotten too complicated. If nothing else, I solved the mystery. Tata Kachora is an amazing person and he was Castaneda's man. But so much time has passed that no clear picture can emerge, even with a lot more research. We can be sure that Tata Kachora is a human treasure and can provide much important information.

The most important thing is that Tata Kachora sees what is happening to the Earth and to us humans. He is her voice.

Please listen.

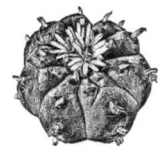

Epilogue
Still Beauty All Around

So we all struggle through this difficult time. It was good fortune to have so many good experiences in this one life! It is summer now and I'm driving home, but to where and why? Almost everything has changed. The woods. My relationship with Gloria. The beauty. There are wildfires and tragedies in California. Many friends are refugees from the fires. And I am a refugee because Tata Kachora was the last thing I had.

But realize there is still beauty all around. Exist in it. Be happy to have lived long enough to see how it all turned out because "We" predicted it.

Arizona is where the monsoons came and put out the fires. Everything is beautiful! Go there.

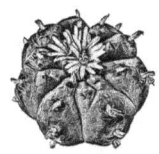

Afterword
Winter Solstice

It was the time of sunrise and I was with my little Tribe in Baja. We were celebrating the occasion at a prehistoric Ceremonial Site. Giant boulders dominated the landscape. Being here with them, in Ceremony, felt good. We were gathered around a cave where the rising sun illuminated a prehistoric painting. It depicted a human figure with roots for legs. Tree of Life? This was our humble Stonehenge.

A moment ago, Mapuche was comfortably leaning back on a flat boulder next to me.

He looked up and said "We made it, Man!"

I understood and answered, "Yeah, that's true."

We made it to old age and are here, celebrating on our terms. No compromises!

Tata Oso and Cecilia were leading the ceremony. They had an urn with smoldering juniper and other ingredients. Oso spoke to us about protecting the Earth and respecting each other. It felt casual.

Using broken Spanish, I spoke briefly about how we are connected to many others in a global movement. We were rediscovering our roots. And like the figure in the cave, our roots are connected to the Earth.

Everyone, except me, had Native American blood and they were all wearing clothes and jewelry that reflected their heritage. Mapuche appeared the most genuine and looked like our tribal elder. Adorned in his jewelry and cool clothes, he could easily pass for an aging Latin American rock star.

Cecelia was the only one here who had grown up in a traditional Native American tribe. Her people never allowed the Catholic Church to destroy their spirituality.

Gloria and I were seeing each other again. She was with her family at their little ranch in Jalisco for the holidays.

It has been almost a year since I met Tata Kachora. Writing about him and the other shamans has given me a purpose.

The next challenge is to market this book. It is a daunting proposition. If this book is widely read, there will probably be a part two. I will happily pay the money in order to write more about Tata Kachora.

I need a reason to continue living. I am afraid!

I love life. I love nature. And I love Gloria. They are all the same force.

Three days later:

It seemed fitting that I was camping in the Southern Arizona desert on Christmas Eve. The gift of rain was here! Life would spring from low spots and from cracks in the big rocks. Babies would be born. It would be a new year.

It was starting to get light in the desert and the rain continued. The camper shell kept me dry as I wrote.

Now, while breaking camp, the sun had come out, creating a rainbow over the mountains. It was a reminder: This is a sacred site.

My Dad conducted a wedding service here about thirty-four years ago. A year later Michelle was born.

It's been so long that over half of the adults who attended are gone now.

Walking through the little valley, I was passing the wedding site. It still looked the same as it did all those years ago. The ironwood trees live hundreds of years and the rocks erode slowly.

It was a little scary in this place. I could see my mom standing in her nice clothes, with the desert behind her, and old Uncle Paul, wearing a brown suit, sipping on a cup of tea. The pictures were in the album to remind me. What else has happened in this stark place? Many things that have been forgotten?

Suddenly there was commotion and a big raptor flew out of a mesquite tree. It looked big enough to be a golden eagle, but I couldn't tell because it was flying away from me. This was a good sign.

There were older spirits here. Many petroglyphs adorned the rocks at this place. It was sacred to the Ancestors.

The Gila River flowed by and people had lived here for thousands of years. This little valley ended where cars raced by on highway 95. The rocks with the petroglyphs towered above. It was a forgotten place.

I write for us to remember.

Notes on mythology and the name Don Juan

Some of us have wondered why Carlos Castaneda chose the name Don Juan for his hero. It may have been because of a connection to European mythology.

A mythological person named Don Juan has been a part of our literature in books, plays and poems, dating all the way back to 1630. (See Wikipedia: Don Juan)

He was a womanizer and sometimes a thief or a trickster.

Castaneda chose the name because it has mystery and power. He may also have been considering his intended readers. During the 1960's, young men like me may have found the title more interesting because it had sexual implications.

Castaneda also may have been giving a nod to Tata Kachora himself. The man was married to two women at the same time when he was a young man. And he has shown a strong and continuing interest in romance; even in my observations. People tell me that he is happy with his new wife.

pelorian digital

www.ingramcontent.com/pod-product-compliance
Lightning Source LLC
Chambersburg PA
CBHW060819190426
43197CB00038B/2127